HOW TO
PUT ON A
MAGIC SHOW
AND MYSTIFY
YOUR FRIENDS
BE A MAGICIAN!

There's more to magic than meets the eye! Dazzle your friends with your sleight-of-hand as you amaze them with hocus-pocus and stupefying feats of magic. Learn how to put on an astonishing magic show from start to finish. Read all about how to use props, music, skits, costumes, and patter to create the best magic show in town. Best of all, some of the sneakiest tricks are explained in detail so you can carry them off like Houdini himself.

Abracadabra! Presto! *Be a Magician!* is more fun than a hat full of rabbits!

BE A

HOW TO PUT ON A MAGIC SHOW AND MYSTIFY YOUR FRIENDS

MAGICIAN!

BY JAY BOYAR

DRAWINGS BY TOM TOLES
PHOTOGRAPHS BY ANNE TURYN

Julian Messner (M) New York

This book is for my brother, Ben.

Manufactured in the United States of America.

Design by Irving Perkins Associates

Library of Congress Cataloging in Publication Data

Boyar, Jay.
Be a magician!

Bibliography: p.
Includes index.
1. Conjuring—Juvenile literature.   I.   Toles,
Tom.   II.   Turyn, Anne.   III.   Title.
GV1548.B66   793.8   80-26799
ISBN 0-671-42273-1

ACKNOWLEDGMENTS

THIS book never would have been written without the guidance and good wishes of many, many people. Thanking all of them adequately would require writing *another* book. I would, however, like to single out just a few particularly helpful people.

Over the years, the many students in my magic classes have been of tremendous inspiration with their bottomless pit of questions and comments. My parents, Louise and Sam Boyar, have also helped with this book in ways too numerous to mention.

I'd like to extend thanks to David Bookbinder for his early encouragement in planning *Be a Magician!* and to Jim Salicrup and David Anthony Kraft for their suggestions and hospitality.

Special thanks are due to my editor, Iris Rosoff, whose patient support and imagination have seemed boundless. To Tom Toles for his marvelous drawings, to Doug Smith for his painstaking proofreading, and to Anne Turyn and Jane Krupp for their fine photographs, many thanks.

Thank you, also, to magician Howard Eldridge for his

aid in compiling this book's appendixes, and, for their gracious support, to the members of Buffalo's Gene Gordon Ring of the International Brotherhood of Magicians.

Someday, I hope to write another book about magic. If any of my readers have any suggestions for that book—or even any questions about *this* one—I hope they will write to me at this address:

Jay Boyar
c/o Iris Rosoff
Julian Messner
Simon & Schuster Building
1230 Avenue of the Americas
New York, NY 10020

CONTENTS

HOW TO
PUT ON A
MAGIC SHOW
AND MYSTIFY
YOUR FRIENDS
BE A MAGICIAN!

INTRODUCTION

WHY do you want to be a magician?

Keep asking yourself that question. It will help you to decide what kind of magician to be and, as you read this book, you'll become an even better magician than you might have been. You'll know where you're going and that'll help you figure out how to get there.

If you're like me, there are probably many reasons why you want to be a magician. One big reason is that it's a lot of fun. Performing miracles is a very exciting business.

Magic is also a wonderful way to enter the world of entertaining and to do it on a workable, personal scale.

It's not surprising, then, that a lot of famous artists and entertainers began as magicians or have had a strong interest in magic. There is no better overall training for an entertainer than to create and design his own magic show.

Orson Welles, who writes, directs, and acts in movies, was—and still is—a terrific magician. As a boy, Woody Allen was an amateur magician, too.

The list includes movie stars like Cary Grant, Steve

Martin, Tony Curtis, Jerry Lewis, and Tom Smothers. Johnny Carson and Dick Cavett are both very accomplished magicians. The list goes on and on.

Since most magic shows are mounted on a relatively small, manageable scale, you must do almost everything yourself. You must develop the skills of an actor or actress in order to perform and speak well on stage. You must be a writer, for there is no one to write your scripts for you. You must select and record your show's music, and you must select, arrange, and, most often, build your props from scratch. You must build and design your set and costume, and you must arrange the lighting on your set.

If you work with animals or assistants, you must train them. In most cases, you must be your own manager and arrange your own publicity. There aren't many other ways I can think of that a young person can get this range of theatrical experience.

A magic show can be almost anything, provided that it has a certain number of tricks in it. You might mix pantomime with magic, or music or humor or a skit or clowning or ventriloquism or dance or whatever else you're interested in that seems to fit.

As you read this book, you'll notice that I try to get you to think about and question everything about putting on a magic show. If you've seen some magic shows already, you might think, "My magic show has to be something like that." But it doesn't have to be at all.

Many chapters in the book may not even apply to the magic show that you eventually decide to do. Just because I have a chapter about magic wands, for instance, doesn't mean that you have to use a magic wand. Your show can be anything you want it to be. This book is just a guide.

Most books on magic are rather like cookbooks. They contain pages and pages of "recipes" for tricks. These books are fine in their place. After all, you need to know the secrets to tricks, and books of that kind help fill that need. Gimmicks and props used in magic tricks are available through magic stores and from magic supply houses via catalog (See Appendix I).

This book is different from most others because it assumes that you have found other ways of learning magic tricks. Although this book does contain the secrets to over a dozen tricks, its main purpose is to help you get the most out of the tricks presented here and those you may already know. In a word, this is a book about showmanship.

A magician doesn't need all that many tricks to get along quite well. A couple of dozen should last you several years. It's all in how you present them. If there is one mistake that most young magicians make, it is that they furiously try to discover the secrets to as many tricks as they can. Concentrate, instead, on developing new, fun ways of presenting just a handful of tricks, and you will be a much more successful magician and entertainer.

This book is written to be *used*, as well as read. The format is quite simple. A basic aspect of magic is discussed in each chapter and then, in most cases, a trick is described that in some way highlights that aspect.

It's expected that you'll actually perform the tricks described and that you'll think about (and act on) the suggestions made as you create your own approach to performing magic. My hope is that if you follow the suggestions made in this book, you'll acquire the skills and habits of thought that a student in any of the many magic classes I have conducted over the years would develop.

A final word: The real place to begin in magic—as in so many other things—is with yourself. Ask yourself what you'd like to see on stage, if you could see anything at all. If you're lucky, you'll find some answers. If you do, then you'll be a magician.

I

THE MAGICIAN

Magic starts with a magician. And before anything else, a magician needs a name, some special words, and an appropriate costume.

The chapters in this section are designed to help you create a character for yourself on stage through a concentration on the areas listed above. These are really just exercises to help you consider what kind of impression you want to make when you perform magic.

These chapters are about finding yourself on stage.

CHAPTER ONE

NAMING YOURSELF

WHEN you are born, you're almost immediately given a name. That name soon becomes the most important word in your life.

People who know nothing else about you know your name. It is a means of instant identification. Although they probably shouldn't, people often make judgments about you on the basis of your name.

When a magician—or any other performer—starts out on stage, it's very important for him to select a name that fits. Sometimes a performer will simply use the name he was born with as his stage name. Frequently, however, a performer will invent another name which more accurately conveys the nature of what he does on stage. This is especially true of magicians.

A magician is a person of mystery, so it may be inappropriate for him or her to use the regular, everyday name in performing magic. In addition to this, there is an old tradition among magicians to end their names in the letter

"I." The great escape artist, Harry Houdini, was actually named Ehrich Weiss. He chose the name Houdini by adding "i" to "Houdin" as in Robert-Houdin, a famous French magician whom Houdini much admired.

The magician called Cardini chose that name because his act is mostly card manipulation. And Slidini is a master of sleight of hand.

Some magicians will just add an "i" to their first or last name and use that as a stage name. Robert Jones, for example, might call himself "Roberti" or "Jonesini." Helen Brown might be "Heleni" or "Brownini."

This method of finding a name begins to seem a little corny or old-fashioned today. More effective, perhaps, would be to select a name from a novel or a poem that strikes you as filled with magic and mystery. It is also crucial that you feel comfortable with the name and that it fit you and your on-stage personality. .

If judged simply on the basis of their stage names, magicians as a group might be considered to be among the most egotistical of people. I say this because they are always adding extremely complimentary adjectives to their names. Blackstone was billed as "The Greatest Magician the World Has Ever Known," while Thurston, another great magician, was known as "Thurston, the World's Greatest Magician."

These rather extreme adjectives might seem embarrassing to a modest person, but try not to let it bother you. Adjectives like "the amazing," "the sensational," and "the great" are just ways performers emphasize that their acts are carnival acts. Magicians, acrobats, sword swallowers, and other carnival performers often use this type of adjective, and it's just a shorthand, really, to let the public know what kind of act to expect. These adjectives function like the titles "Capt." or "Dr." or "Rev.," which give you a clue to the occupation of the person you are addressing.

Think of it this way: It's all part of the illusion you are creating. If you really could perform the miracles you only *seem* to do, then an adjective like great would be quite accurate.

WHAT'S IN A NAME?

The effect: The magician displays several cards, each of which contains one letter of his name. The magician predicts which of the letters will be selected by a spectator.

The trick: Holding several cards in his hand, the magician addresses the audience saying, "Audiences seem to have a horrible problem remembering the names of the performers they see. This is very hard on the performer, since after working very hard doing a show, he would like his audience to at least remember who he is."

As he speaks, the magician begins placing the cards on a small rack, with the backs of the cards facing the audience. "To solve this problem, I have had these calling cards made with my name on them." The magician begins turning the cards around one by one so that they are revealed to the audience. The audience will usually find this somewhat amusing, because each calling card only has one letter of the magician's name on it. (Ordinarily, a calling card contains a person's entire name.)

Let's assume that the magician's name is Houdini. In this case, there would be seven cards, with one letter on each.

The magician selects a volunteer from the audience and inquires as to that volunteer's name. Then the magician asks the spectator to freely choose any one of the cards and hold it up in full view of everyone.

Suppose the spectator picks up the "N." The magician explains that he has written on a piece of paper a prediction about the letter he thought that the spectator would pick and that that paper is, let us say, under a book on the magician's table. At the magician's request, the spectator lifts up the book and under it is a piece of paper on which is written "N." This will work, no matter which letter the spectator chooses.

The secret: This is a very simple trick to do, but it can have an extremely powerful effect on an audience. It also has the added benefit of actually helping the spectators remember your name.

Before you start, make cards, each of which has one letter of your name on it. It would be a good idea to take some care in making these cards so that they are as attractive as possible. They are, in a sense, your calling cards.

Then take several pieces of paper and write one letter of your name on each one. If your name were Houdini, you would need seven cards but only six pieces of paper. That is, you should make one card for each letter, but one piece of paper for each *different* letter. Since the "I" occurs twice in Houdini, you'd have cards with "H," "O," "U," "D," "I," "N," and "I" on them, and pieces of paper with "H," "O," "U," "D," "I," and "N" on them.

Take these pieces of paper and conceal them in different places throughout the room. Put one under a book, one under a chair cushion, and so on. You must remember where these papers are hidden.

When the trick is performed, no matter which letter the spectator selects, have her go to the spot in the room where the slip of paper with that particular letter on it is hidden. The audience will assume that that slip of paper is the only one you've prepared, and they will be quite amazed at your powers of prognostication.

Variation: This trick is easily adapted to many situations. If you were doing a show at a birthday party, you could use the birthday boy or girl's name rather than your own. If you were doing a show for a holiday party (say, a Halloween party), you could use the letters of that holiday's name. You might even forget about letters completely and use symbols or pictures. Commonly used magic symbols include a star, a cross, three wavy lines, a circle, a square, and a triangle. Just use your imagination!

CHAPTER TWO

MAGIC WORDS

OF all the words a magician uses in performing a magic trick, the most important ones are the so-called magic words. These are the words the magician speaks at the climax of a trick, the incantations which supposedly make the incredible feat of magic happen.

Familiar magic words include hocus-pocus, abracadabra, and presto. Many magicians rely on these words exclusively because the words are already associated, in the mind of the public, with magic. A magician must create the illusion that the moment when the magic word is spoken is the moment that the trick actually happens. In reality, most tricks have had their tricky parts accomplished long before the magic word is said. By making the audience think that the magic takes place when you say "hocus-pocus" (or whatever), it further disguises how the trick is actually done.

Sometimes it is a good idea to stick to established magic words like those mentioned above, because they already seem very magical to most people. But other times, you might want to make up magic words of your own.

You may notice that most magic words sound pretty strange. This peculiarity helps to make them seem more magical. When you are making up your own magic words, it will help if you make them sound strange and mysterious.

One way to do that is to write a familiar word backward. For instance, the word paper sounds very plain, but by reversing the order of the letters, you get "repap." You might want to make up a rhyming magic word combination like, say, "repap-kepap." The word magic itself is "cigam," which could be a pretty effective word if used in a trick.

Perhaps you'd like to use the reverse of your own name. If your name is Susan, your magic word might be "na-sus." If Michael is your name, then use the word "leah-cim." You might want to combine magical words together to form a mysterious-sounding magical chant. Using the magic words we have invented, plus a few others, you could create a chant like:

> Cigam, cigam, repap-kepap.
> Na-sus, Leah-cim, cigam tep.
> Re-pap, re-pap, cigam kepap.
> Leah-cim, Leah-cim, cigam rep.

Another approach is to invent magic words to fit a specific trick. For instance, if you were doing a trick that involved making a cut rope whole again, you could devise a nutty word that sounded like rope; "rope-allah," for instance. If you were doing a trick that involved silk handkerchiefs, you might say "silkola."

Using a chant—instead of just a magic word—has the advantage of sounding darker and more mysterious. However, if you use a simple magic word, you could ask the whole audience to join you in saying it.

Suppose you decide to use the word "na-sus." You'd want the whole audience to repeat it after you, so—after telling everyone what the word is—you might say, "Okay. Now when I say three, everyone please say the magic word with me. Ready? One, two, three, na-sus!" That way, everyone says the word together.

Very often, a magician is called upon to perform for a special occasion. Sometimes it isn't a bad idea to devise a magic word especially for that occasion. Let's say you're performing at a birthday party. Instead of saying "hocus-pocus," it might be appropriate to simply say "happy birthday" to cause the magic to happen. At a Christmas party, the words "jingle bells" would be effective. If you perform at a school or for a club, then the name of that school or that club would be a good choice, especially if you asked the entire audience to shout it with you.

Sometimes, if you ask the audience to shout out the magic word and they don't say it very loudly or they don't say it altogether, you could pretend that the trick hasn't worked yet and ask them to try saying it again, but louder this time. This will add to the fun by increasing the suspense and making the group feel that it is really helping to do the trick. It will also further the illusion that the trick is actually occurring at the moment that the word is being spoken.

Of course, nobody believes that saying a magic word will cause a rabbit to appear in a hat or turn a white silk handkerchief black, but you'd be surprised how willing an audience is to temporarily enter into a world of imagination where such things can actually happen. No one is really taken in, but everyone wants to play along.

THE CIRCLE OF MYSTERY

The effect: A spectator writes a secret word on a piece of paper. The paper is destroyed, and the magician divines the word.

The trick: This illusion is unique in that it asks the spectator, rather than the magician, to invent a magic word. A spectator is chosen, and the magician hands him or her a pencil and a plain piece of paper, 5" x 6", with a circle drawn in the middle of it.

"So often," the magician says, "do we magicians find ourselves using magic words that it's not surprising to discover that the magic powers these words contain get used up pretty quickly. I've almost completely exhausted hocus-pocus and abracadabra for this month, and I'd better not try using presto until February, if I know what's good for me.

"Finding new magic words is something I'm always trying to do, so I'd like you to help me," the magician continues, turning to the spectator with the paper and pencil. "Please write any word you like in the circle on the paper you have. Any word at all, as long as it's clean. You could write the name of the street you live on, a friend's first name, your favorite class in school, or a word you make up. That will be the magic word. Write it in the circle, but don't let me see it."

When this has been accomplished, the magician instructs the spectator to fold the paper twice, so that the word can't be seen. Then the spectator is asked to hand the folded paper to the magician.

The magician then tears the paper into tiny pieces and places them in an ashtray. He goes to get some matches and then lights the pieces, letting them burn until they are just ashes. (Remember to be very careful with the matches.)

"Now comes the difficult part," the performer announces. "I'd like to ask that everyone concentrate very hard on the magic word that was selected, and I'll see if I can pick up the thought waves and tell you what it is." The audience concentrates and, abracadabra, the magician can tell them the exact word selected.

The secret: Before the trick starts, take a piece of plain 5″ x 6″ paper and fold it twice so that firm creases are

FIGURE A

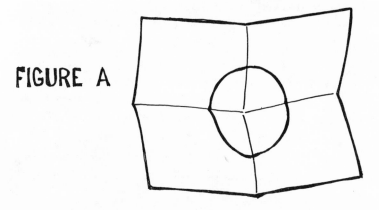

FIGURE B

made. Open the paper up, and on the inside draw a circle in the middle, about 2″ in diameter (Figure A). Hand this paper and a pencil to the spectator as the trick begins. Proceed as outlined above.

When the time comes for the spectator to fold up the paper, have him fold it on the creases you have already made. This means that the magic word will be on a very small corner of the paper where the folds meet (Figure B). When you tear up the paper, tear it so that you don't tear up the folded circle, and so that the little corner of the paper that contains the circle is always kept at the very back of the pieces of paper, closest to your chest. When it comes time for you to place the pieces of paper in an ashtray, smoothly slide the corner containing the circle into the palm of your hand. Then, when you turn to get some matches, secretly open up that little piece of paper and read the word inside. Then dispose of the paper behind a prop or in a box. Now that you know what the magic word is, you can proceed with the rest of the trick as outlined above.

Variation: Some magicians might like to have the spectator write a number or draw a little picture in the circle, instead of having him pick a magic word. If it's a small party (a dozen people or so), you could ask the spectator to write the name of some person at the party in the circle.

Hint: Do this trick first in your act, and then, throughout the rest of the act, use the magic word selected by the spectator as the magic word in the tricks that follow.

CHAPTER THREE

YOUR COSTUME

S you go about your everyday life, you are constantly making judgments and being judged on the basis of clothing. Should you see a person in a white coat with a stethoscope around her neck, you immediately assume that she's a doctor. A man in trunks with big gloves on his hands is identified as a boxer.

What is true in general is even more applicable to the stage. Actors and actresses take great care in selecting just the right clothing to tell the audience the right things about the personalities of the characters they are playing. In the normal course of your life, you often have hours, days, or even years to convey information about yourself to the people in your life. But on stage, you have just a couple of hours (at the most) to make an impression. It's no wonder that great care is taken in designing the wardrobes of characters in plays.

It has often been said that a magician is an actor who plays the same role for his entire life: He plays the role of a magician. Because of this, a magician must be even more careful about his wardrobe than an actor. An actor changes costumes with every play. But once a magician has established a costume, he or she may make no drastic changes in it for years, if ever.

In developing your costume, you should avoid being too rigid at first. Try out different types of magic costumes until you fix on one that is best for you.

When you do find a costume you like, you should try to stay with it. It will become a part of your trademark, like your name. As soon as people see you on stage, dressed as a magician, they will immediately put themselves in a frame of mind that will be especially receptive to the miracles you intend to perform.

The main thing to keep in mind when designing your costume is that it should look different from the clothing you ordinarily wear. It should look *special*. Sometimes all this means is wearing a brightly colored scarf around your neck with your normal street clothes. It could mean wearing a false moustache (or a real one when you're old enough). It could mean placing a hat on your head. A costume can be as simple or elaborate as you choose. The main thing is that when people see you on stage, they should immediately begin to guess that you are going to do something unusual. Whatever costume you invent that accomplishes that effect will do just fine.

I'm going to describe several different kinds of costumes that you might want to consider. I do not want to recommend that you adopt any of these, exactly. They are only described to suggest some of the costumes that

Humorous trickster Dave Evans tries some impromptu coin magic with a pencil as a makeshift wand. His "costume" is pretty ordinary —except, of course, for the rabbit ears.

have been tried by other magicians so that you have a clearer idea of where you can begin when you come to design your own costume.

THE TRADITIONAL COSTUME. To most people a magician is a man in formal evening attire: a tuxedo, a top hat, a black bow tie, and a wand. He has a dark moustache or a goatee, and he is very dramatic in his speech and movements.

A modified version of this could be made by simply dressing up in your nicest suit (or a sports jacket and dressy pants) with a bow tie. You could get a false moustache and a cheap top hat from a novelty store. (They now sell stiff cardboard and plastic ones that look pretty convincing.) Magicians rarely wear top hats these days, but you could start your show wearing it and then, as you bow to the audience, remove it and place it on a table for the rest of the time. Your initial impression will carry the air of magic throughout the performance, even though you've removed the hat.

You might want to put a dark cape around your shoulders. A cape can easily be made from an old sheet dyed black and pinned (with safety pins) to the lapels of your coat.

THE GYPSY. Gypsies are known for their magic spells and curses, so a gypsy outfit is very adaptable for a magician. Also, many girls who do magic feel uncomfortable in a traditionally male top hat and tails and would feel much more relaxed in a gypsy costume. You should wear a long skirt that is colorful to the point of being gaudy. Wrap a bandanna (a scarf) around your head and one around your waist.

Wear plenty of jewelry: necklaces, earrings, finger rings, bracelets, and so on. You could even carry a tambourine, which you might bang every time you do a magic trick.

THE CLOWN. Many clowns perform magic and many magicians dress as clowns. There are any number of ways to make yourself clownlike. You could wear a loosely fitting, colorful costume, perhaps using modified pajamas. Or, wear a tattered suit and be a tramp clown. A bowler hat (this, too, is available cheaply in plastic and cardboard versions from novelty stores) might crown a hobo clown, or perhaps a fright wig. You will want to make up your face colorfully, and a large red nose is almost a must. For this, you could use a hollow red rubber ball, cut open to grip your nose. If there is a lot of humor, especially physical humor, in your act, you might want to seriously consider a clown costume.

THE SWAMI. India is shrouded in a mystique of magic and mystery. A *fakir* in India is a worker of miracles. He might charm snakes by playing a flute. He might cause a coil of rope to rise magically as a thin strand into the air, climb it, and—when he reached the top—disappear. He'd probably wear no more than a loincloth, which would be rather inappropriate—and cold—for a magician performing in a Western country.

A modified version of this Swami outfit could be dark pants, a dark turtleneck shirt, and a white turban, made

Usually, a magician in a top hat and tuxedo magically produces white doves. In a reversal of standard procedure, a giant white dove (Bob Little) produces small, tuxedo-clad magicians.

by folding a sheet around your head. A brooch should be pinned to the center-front of the turban. Another brooch should be pinned to your shirt (in the vicinity of the center of your chest) or worn on a chain around your neck. Once again, a beard or a moustache might be appropriate or, perhaps, a single earring.

THE ORIENTAL MAGICIAN. The Orient, like India, is considered an exotic land where magic is everywhere, just below the surface of things.

An oriental costume can be easily created by wearing a bathrobe. In fact, many clothing stores sell kimono-style bathrobes which are just perfect. A long, thin moustache is also in order if you're a boy, and your hair (if it is long) should be pulled back in a tight bun. You could wear sandals on your feet and use a chopstick to do your magic, instead of a magic wand.

There is an endless variety of possible costumes. The main thing is to create one in which you feel the most like a magician. If your costume is fairly neutral (by which I mean, if it is rather like conventional street clothes), you might wear various costumes throughout your show, each costume fitting the trick you are performing.

THE ORIENTAL TUBE OF PLENTY

The effect: A tube is shown to be empty and is then covered on both ends. A moment later, the tube is magically filled with all kinds of colorful cloths and streamers.

The trick: A magician, in an oriental costume, addresses the audience. "I'd like to show you an illusion I learned when I was traveling in the Orient. This illusion is very popular there, where people love colorful lanterns, scarves, and banners," says the magician. He holds up a tube that is covered on one end with a tissue paper. The audience can see the tube is empty.

"This is a tube of the sort that Oriental magicians use rather like we use suitcases. Suppose you wanted to travel somewhere and bring your belongings with you, but you didn't want to strain yourself lugging a heavy suitcase everywhere you went. Well, if you had one of these, your problems would be over. Just cover the other end of it like this," says the magician, as he covers the other end with a tissue paper. He makes a magic pass over the tube with his wand (a chopstick). Then he breaks one of the tissue seals, and endless silk handkerchiefs, banners, and streamers emerge from the tube. Some of the handkerchiefs have large oriental dragons painted on them. The effect is spectacular.

The secret: Take a cardboard tube that is around 7" tall and 4" in diameter, and paint it bright yellow. You could use a tube in which Quaker Oats cereal comes or any other tube of these approximate dimensions. Yellow spray paint is good for coloring the tube. Be sure you coat it completely and evenly. Then, on what might be called the front and back, paint Chinese characters as in Figure A. Paint these in black paint, and they will give the trick a real oriental feeling. If possible, the inside of the tube should also be painted black.

FIGURE A

FIGURE B

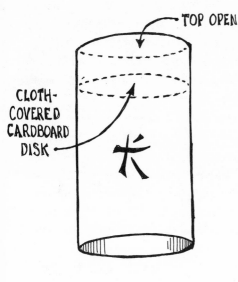

TOP OPEN

CLOTH-
COVERED
CARDBOARD
DISK

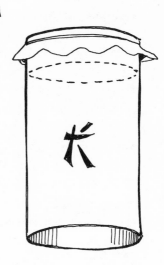

You will also want to get a good supply of paper towels or napkins. A good color to use is red. It looks attractive with yellow and also shows up very well when the trick is performed.

Take a paper towel and tape it in place, 1½"–2" from one end of the tube, so that when you look in through the other end you see a flat sheet of red paper towel. You should then cut a circle of thin cardboard just slightly smaller in diameter than the tube and tape it next to the paper towel between the paper towel and the end of the tube closest to the paper towel.

Next, on top of the cardboard, load as many neatly folded silk handkerchiefs and rolled streamers as you possibly can. You will be surprised how many will fit. Some of the silks might be painted with oriental dragons or letters; these can be obtained from novelty shops.

Top the whole thing with a red paper towel which is held to the tube by a rubber band slid down over the outside (Figure B). When looked at from the other end of the tube, it appears to be simply an empty tube with a paper towel held on one end with a rubber band.

Start the trick with the tube set up this way, and the audience will think it is empty. Put another paper towel on the other end with another rubber band. Put the tube down for a second and pick up your magic chopstick. When you pick up the tube again, give it a little spin so that the audience won't remember which end was covered at the start. But make sure you remember.

Set the tube down on a table with that end—the loaded end—facing up. Make a magic pass with the chopstick and then puncture the paper towel with it. To the utter amazement of the audience, you will now be able to pull endless handkerchiefs and streamers from the tube. You should drape these openly all around the stage, so it will seem like more items have been pulled out of the tube than could ever fit in it. Perhaps some tiny wrapped candies could also be withdrawn and given to spectators who have helped you with previous tricks. If this is the final trick you are doing in a show, you could have a silk handkerchief made with Chinese characters on one side and the words "The End" on the other side. Pull this last one from the tube and hold it up with the Chinese characters facing the audience. Smile and then turn it over so that they see it is the end of your show.

II TOOLS OF THE TRADE

New tricks demand new tools and new props. And they can become very expensive.

But a magic show doesn't have to cost a lot. The illusions described in this book, for example, can all be made easily, with inexpensive materials.

This section explains how to make your own magic wand, the most commonly used prop. It also discusses the magician's cards.

In this section's first chapter, props in general are taken up and some basic rules about them are laid down.

CHAPTER FOUR

PROPS

TECHNICALLY, a prop is anything an actor holds in his hand. In a play, an actor will often go for an entire performance and only be required to use a few props. A magician, however, is constantly making use of props and will use a great many of them in a typical trick.

For an audience, much of the allure of a magic show comes from looking at the fascinating props resting on the magician's table. As a general rule, it is best to leave the props displayed all around your stage on tables before actually using them for a trick. As you perform your opening tricks, the audience will be curious about the other props it sees displayed, and that curiosity will continue to build as the show goes on. The spectators will begin to imagine their own uses for the props they see and will be doubly surprised when you use them in entirely unsuspected ways.

You may want to cover some of your props with opaque cloths. If examined too closely, certain props may reveal secrets. Instead of displaying them too openly, place them on tables, but cover them with cloths. Some props may be so sensitive that you won't want to display them at all. Keep them behind the scenes on a rear table or in a box.

Basically there are two types of props a magician uses: gimmicked and ungimmicked.

A gimmicked prop is one that has something tricky about it. It's a prop that isn't exactly what it seems. It may be a top hat with a false bottom or a playing card with a face on each side.

An ungimmicked prop is one that is exactly what it seems. A hat that is really just a hat, a playing card that is ordinary, and so on.

A good general rule in making and buying props is: If the prop is gimmicked, make it look as ordinary as possible, and if a prop is ungimmicked, make it look special.

There is a sound principle behind this rule. If a prop is gimmicked, you want to arouse as little suspicion about it as you can manage. Making it look as plain and ordinary as possible helps the audience to accept it for what it appears to be.

On the other hand, if a prop has nothing tricky about it, you make it look special to divert suspicion from the tricky props and to arouse a general sense of mystery and amazement about what you're doing. If there is nothing gimmicked about the prop, you can always let the audience examine it.

Some props that are intriguing to look at may be placed around your set, even if they have no real relation to any tricks you are doing. A decorated box or an imaginatively shaped glass or bottle can help give your stage an air of mystery.

Card manipulation expert Walt Cummings demonstrates an elaborate card fan.

If you are doing a trick that involves telling a story, it could work well to add some props that help create the setting of the story. Perhaps you do a trick that talks about a cook whose dishes always disappear. You might work some cooking instruments—like a ladle or a measuring cup—into the trick just for color.

If you are using a gimmicked prop, you must be very careful what you say about it. If, for example, you are using a trick deck of cards, you'll want the audience to believe that it is an ordinary deck of cards. The worst thing you could say to the audience, however, is, "This is an ordinary deck of cards."

Saying that increases the suspicion in the mind of the listener that the deck may not be ordinary. A better approach would be to riffle the deck, so the audience can see it, and then to extract the jokers from it before you proceed. The audience, seeing you extract the jokers, will believe the deck is ordinary and untampered with. They will think, "He didn't even take the time to extract the jokers before coming on stage. The deck probably was one he just picked up and brought on stage with him."

As discussed in Chapter Five, the magic wand is usually the magician's most important prop, the one that seems to cause all the magic to happen. However, you might not want to use a wand at all, or you might want to have alternate magical props.

A large, shiny stone or gem (perhaps a piece of costume jewelry) can be an effective magical charm or amulet. A colorful ring of metal or plastic might seem to an audience to have potent mystical properties. Think carefully about this, because, from the audience's viewpoint, it may seem to be the most important part of your illusion.

The magical props are seldom gimmicked and can usually be handled pretty casually without a trick being revealed or an important gimmick falling apart. However, it is very important to handle all magical props as if they were really magical: carefully, lovingly, and cautiously. This will help create the illusion among the audience that the prop really is a powerful charm.

Conversely, the gimmicked props that look like ordinary objects should be handled as undramatically and as casually as possible. You should be careful not to inadvertently expose a trick's secret.

Keep all your props in good working order, repairing or replacing any that have become broken or damaged through use. A workman, the saying goes, is only as good as his tools.

WHICH ONE?

The effect: A tray containing 10 unusual objects is displayed. One object is secretly selected by a spectator. The magician is able to magically determine which object was selected.

The trick: On a tray displayed to the audience are 10 or so objects, each of which is an odd version of something familiar. For example, if a clock is used, then it must be a rather ornate and strange-looking clock. These will be objects that you gather over a period of time by browsing through garage sales, flea markets, Goodwill counters, old attics, etc.

"On this tray are 10 mysterious objects I have gathered in my many travels around the world," the magician explains, displaying the tray. "Here is a clock from the chamber of Confucius, which was smuggled out of China by a thief. This, over here, is a cut-glass goblet which, it is said, was the favorite wine glass of the French leader, Napoleon, when he relaxed during his many bloody campaigns. . . ." In this manner, the magician continues pointing out each object on the tray and telling a tall tale connected with each one.

"One of these objects must be selected without my knowing which one. This must be done very carefully to avoid the possibility of secret agreement—knowingly or unknowingly—between myself and any member of the audience," the magician continues.

"I'll randomly pass these pieces of paper to some of you." With this, the magician passes 20 or so small pieces of paper and pencils to audience members at random. She then asks the people with paper to write down the name of one object (clock, glass, etc.) that they see on the tray.

The audience is then instructed to fold the papers twice so that what has been written down is hidden from view.

At this point, the magician takes a plain brown paper bag, opens it up, and says, "I finished my lunch earlier, so luckily we've got this bag to collect the papers. Would you all place your papers in this bag?"

Then, holding onto the bag, the magician goes to each person who has a piece of paper, has the person drop the paper in the bag, and thanks him or her. (The magician, in so doing, also remembers to take back the pencils from the people in the free hand and to discard them.)

"Now, to prevent any hanky-panky, I'd like to ask *you*," says the magician, picking another spectator at random, "to reach into the bag and pick out one and only one piece of paper." The magician holds the bag above the head of that person, so he can't have any visual control over which piece of paper is selected.

"Without looking at it, hand the folded paper to someone else," says the magician, and the volunteer complies.

"Now I will concentrate, and perhaps I will be able to tell you which of the objects was picked." With eyes shut, the magician concentrates, and finally says, "I see armies marching across a battlefield. I see a French flag and a clever leader. It's Napoleon's glass."

She opens her eyes and, very deliberately, walks over to the tray and lifts the glass up high. "Please open the paper and read what is written there," says the magician.

The spectator with the paper opens it up and reads out loud, "glass."

The secret: To do this trick, select 10 objects and put them on a tray. There is nothing gimmicked about any of them, but they look very unusual so that they will attract attention and divert it from the one genuinely tricky prop in the illusion: the paper bag.

Before you start the trick, glue (using rubber cement) a flap, made from the side of another identical bag, into the paper bag, as in Figure A. Inside this flap (Area X), put about 20 double-folded slips of paper, all of which say "glass." Get 20 unfolded, blank pieces of paper which are otherwise identical to those in the bag. You are ready.

Proceed as outlined above. When you display the paper bag, casually show the inside with the flap covering the hidden "glass" papers in Area X.

FIGURE A

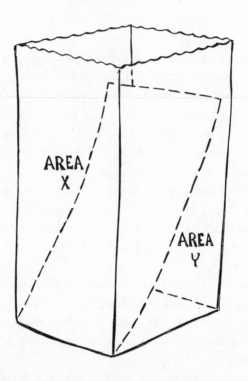

AREA
X

AREA
Y

Have the audience members put their papers in the empty pocket (Area Y), and when all of them are in, secretly flip the flap uncovering the special "glass" papers. You hold the bag above the head of the spectator who selects the paper so that he will not see exactly what has happened. Any paper he selects from the "glass" paper pouch (Area X) will say "glass" on it. Since you know this, it will be no problem for you to "sense" which object has been selected.

CHAPTER FIVE

MAGIC WANDS

HEN you think of a magician, the first thing that comes to mind is a rabbit, the second is a top hat, and the third is a wand.

Today, many magicians have discarded their top hats (too old-fashioned) and their rabbits (too troublesome). But, somehow, the wand remains.

There are reasons for this. In the first place, a wand is very versatile and adaptable to almost any kind of magic trick. Its very presence brings an air of mystery, amazement, and imagination to a trick. It is also a way performers instantly identify themselves in the minds of the audience as a magician.

What I mean is this: If you see a person coming up your walk with a saw or a screwdriver in her hand, you might immediately guess that she's a carpenter. If he's carrying a bag of letters, you'd strongly suspect that he's a mailman. So, the minute you see a performer with a wand, you begin to expect something magical to happen.

53

Another reason that so many magicians use wands is that wands are very practical in performing tricks. In most tricks, a wand—while appearing to be magical—is actually the most ordinary prop the magician uses.

For example, suppose you're doing a trick that uses a bag with a special secret compartment. You wouldn't want your audience to notice that compartment since it is secret (and perhaps you have some silk handkerchiefs hidden in it). In order to get the audience to think of the bag as ordinary, you might use a common-looking, brown paper bag. You might handle it casually and hardly even look at it.

But, since the audience knows that something magical is going to happen, you've got to give them something magical to look at, so that they don't watch the bag too closely.

This is where the wand comes in. If it looks magical, and if you hold it and move it mysteriously, the audience will forget about the bag and concentrate on the wand. A wand is also a valuable tool for directing a spectator's attention precisely where you want him or her to look. The slender, sticklike shape of a magic wand has the uncanny ability to direct attention wherever you care to point it.

A wand is also helpful in other ways. Suppose you have a coin placed on a table, behind a small box, so the audience can't see it. And suppose, in doing a trick, you have to secretly pick up that coin and hold it in your hand.

Now, if you tried to do that by just sneaking around and picking up the coin without looking in that direction, the audience, 9 times out of 10, would still notice the movement of your hand, and the trick would be spoiled. But if you were to place the wand on the table right next to the coin, then you could openly and deliberately pick up the wand to use in some magical hocus-pocus, and while you were at it, secretly pick up the coin, too, without anyone ever catching on.

I might add that if you are not especially experienced at standing up before a group of people, you may find it hard to know what to do with your hands. A wand gives you something to do with them that seems natural. Just make sure you don't twiddle it nervously as you speak. Hold it firmly, like a precious, valued charm.

Wands are available cheaply from magic stores and through magical supply catalogs. But it is usually more fun—and quite easy—to make your own wand.

First, you have to decide what you want your wand to look like. The traditional magic wand is black with white tips on each end. This works well because its contrasts are eye-catching. However, other colors work well, too, and may be more in keeping with your own personality as a performer. Red is a good, vivid color to use in a wand; so are gold and silver. Any bright color seems to work. You may want to put designs or shapes like stars or half-moons on your wand, instead of the usual contrasting tips. I know of at least one magician whose wand was striped, like a barber's pole.

Keeping in mind that many variations are possible, I'll explain one way to make a traditional magic wand. You'll need a dowel that is about ⅜″ in diameter. You can get one at any hardware store. These dowels are generally pretty long, so you'll have to saw off part of it so that it's about 16″ long. After sawing, you may want to use some sandpaper to smooth off the rough end.

Get a can of black spray paint and spray the whole dowel until it's all black (or whatever color you've chosen). Let it dry. If you miss any spots, spray it again. You can always touch it up with a black magic marker.

Next, get some white plastic tape, 1½″ across. You can get this at most stationery stores; many hardware stores have it, too. Wrap a strip of tape around each tip of the wand. When you're done, you'll have a magic wand that will last you for years.

If you are called upon unexpectedly to do some magic tricks at a friend's house or at a party, you will probably not have your magic wand with you. In that case, almost anything can serve as a makeshift wand. A pencil or a pen is a good impromptu wand. Chopsticks make good wands, and so do butter knives. The important thing is that whatever you choose, use it and handle it as if it were invested with magical powers. Don't let anyone handle it carelessly. Why, the last time I let someone hold my magic wand, he turned into a frog! It took most of the rest of the day to turn him back into a human being.

THE FLOATING RING

The effect: A borrowed ring is made to float up and down the length of a magic wand.

The trick: The magician tells the audience that electro-magnetic waves are all around us and that if we can harness them temporarily, we can use that power to work miracles. She might also hint that the government is at work on research to refine the process, and if the experiments are successful, it could end the energy shortage.

In order to demonstrate this principle, the magician borrows a finger ring from an audience member. (Just in case no one in the audience has a ring, you might want to carry one with you to use in an emergency.)

"In order to use the electromagnetic waves surrounding us," the magician explains, "it's necessary to have a light-ning rod. This magic wand will make an excellent lightning rod." And, with that, the magician pulls the wand from her back pocket and shows it to the audience.

Next, with the left hand, she holds the wand at the bottom, perpendicular to the floor, and, with the right hand, places the ring over the top so that it slides down the wand onto the left hand. With her right hand, the magician moves the ring up and down to demonstrate what she'd like the electric current to do to the ring. Finally, she allows it to rest where it had been, near the bottom of the wand on the left hand.

Then, at the magician's signal, the ring begins to float upward, stopping at any position on the wand that the magician points at with her right hand. The magician keeps this up for a few minutes, playing with the ring, the wand, and those "electromagnetic currents."

At last, with a flourish, the ring jumps off the wand al-together and lands in the magician's right hand. Both the ring and the wand can be passed to the audience for examination.

The secret: This trick is unusual in that its secret is actually contained in the magic wand. Usually, there is nothing tricky about the wand itself, but in this case, there is. You should attach a piece of black thread to the top of the wand. If you make a wand like the one I've described, you could use a piece of the same white plastic tape to attach the thread to the wand. Otherwise, you could use a small piece of clear tape or a bit of wax. You will have to experiment to see how long the piece of thread should be. The other end of the thread is attached to a button on your blouse or shirt or to a belt loop on your pants.

It is best if you wear dark clothing for this trick, so that the thread will be invisible when you do it. You will find that against dark clothing, a slender black thread is not visible to an audience at a distance of a few feet.

As the trick begins, the wand is in your back pocket. When you pull it out, hold the end on which the thread is attached, in your right hand and wave it around a little.

When you get ready to put the ring on it, you are holding the end of the wand without the thread attached to it in your left hand. You put the ring over the wand *and* the thread together (Figure A). If the thread is slack, the ring will drop down onto your left hand. But as you move the wand away from your body (keeping it perpendicular to the floor), the thread will get taut and the ring will begin to rise. You can easily control just how much it will rise and sink by varying the distance the wand is from your body (Figure B).

FIGURE A

FIGURE B

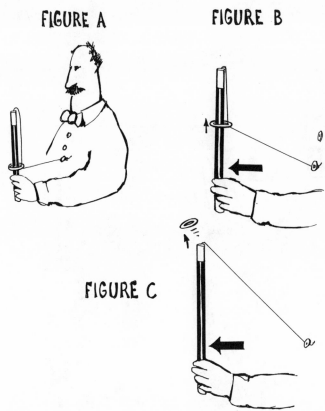

FIGURE C

For the climax of the trick, give the wand a sharp snap as you pull it away from you, and the ring will fly off the wand (Figure C). You should practice catching the ring in your right hand. This motion will mask the fact that as you pull the wand away from your body you pull the thread off the wand and it dangles unnoticed against your clothing. Now both the wand and the ring are entirely ordinary and can be examined. But if you let someone from the audience examine the wand, tell her to be very careful or she might accidentally do some strange magic trick that could alarm everyone. (We have our illusions to maintain, after all.)

CHAPTER SIX

MAGIC WITH CARDS

S INCE so many magic tricks involve cards, it's a good idea to look a little more closely at the cards themselves.

It's commonly known that a standard deck of playing cards contains 52 cards divided into four suits: hearts, diamonds, spades, and clubs. Each suit contains an ace, numbers 2–10, a jack, a queen, and a king. Sometimes, a joker or two is thrown in.

Cards were not always this standardized. At different times throughout the centuries in different countries, decks of cards have contained a variety of numbers, characters, and configurations. In contrast, today it is very hard to find a deck of playing cards (with the exception of children's cards and pinochle decks) that is not arranged as described above.

Decks are usually found in two sizes: the poker deck, which is 3½" long and 2½" across, and the bridge deck, which is also 3½" long but only 2¼" wide. Most magicians prefer the bridge deck, because its sleeker shape allows more control when doing tricky maneuvers with the cards.

Magic tricks with cards often do not work out very well with a large audience. It is hard to see the numbers on small playing cards from a back seat in an auditorium. Some magicians have attempted to solve this problem by buying huge decks of cards measuring 7″ x 5″ and larger. That kind of deck, however, limits the kind of tricks you can do. You certainly can't palm a card the size of a magazine.

Performing card tricks for young children can sometimes present problems. Children often don't know their numbers well enough to understand card tricks. You can minimize these problems by using cards with animals or different colors on them, instead of the standard decks. Children will recognize and remember a giraffe more easily than a six of spades.

Since many tricks involve the spectator shuffling the cards, it should be noted that children's hands are often too small to do that smoothly. When you are performing for children, choose tricks that do not involve the audience handling the cards extensively. In fact, the best rule of thumb is to keep the card tricks to a minimum when youngsters are present.

The best setting for card tricks is a small, informal group of people seated around a table. The best kind of deck to use is a borrowed deck. If you are with a group of friends who ask you to do a trick unexpectedly and you borrow a deck of cards and perform, it is much more impressive than if you do such a trick on stage. On stage, the audience knows that you had all the time in the world to prepare the cards in some special way. As a matter of fact, unless you use a borrowed deck, an audience will always assume that the deck a magician uses is a trick, gimmicked deck, even if it isn't and even if the magician allows the audience to examine it.

Many magicians *do* use gimmicked decks, and sometimes the effect achieved with such a deck is so startling that its worth the risk of using a trick deck. Many gimmicked decks look like normal decks to the untrained eye.

Trick decks are manufactured in all kinds of designs and styles, but the most common one is in the Aviator style. Because of this, most magicians use cards of this style, to avoid suspicion if they switch from using a normal (or "straight") deck to using a gimmicked one. If you are casual about switching from deck to deck, the audience will think that you are still using the original deck, after you've switched to the tricky one.

Magicians often use what are called "pet" decks. A pet deck is a deck that is the same style as another deck, except that the pattern on the back side of the cards is a different color. Red and blue Aviator decks, for instance, might be used in a trick where both the spectator and the magician use decks of cards (like the trick described later in this chapter). The magician might use the blue one, while the spectator uses the red one.

A "stacked" deck is an ordinary deck that has been secretly prearranged so that the cards are in some special order known only to the magician.

One point that many people overlook about card tricks

is that, while they can be among the most fascinating kinds of magic, they can also be quite boring to watch. It all depends on how the tricks are done.

If you know 1,000 ways of figuring out what card the spectator has selected and only one way of announcing to him or her what the card is, then as far as the audience is concerned, you know only one card trick. On the other hand, if you know only one way of figuring out which card has been selected, but 1,000 ways of revealing that card to the spectator, it will seem like you know 1,000 card tricks. And, in a way, you do.

AMATEUR MAGICIAN

The effect: The magician and the spectator each select a card from a different deck. Amazingly, the spectator is

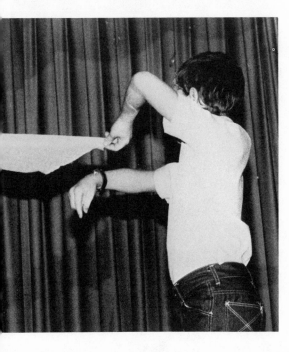

Magician Mack Picknick and two young helpers attempt an illusion using a long scarf as a prop.

able to locate the magician's card, and the magician is able to locate the spectator's card. By an incredible coincidence, both cards turn out to be the same.

The trick: The magician has two decks, a red-backed deck and a blue-backed deck. He puts them both face down on the table and asks the spectator to select one deck. The spectator does so, and the magician takes the other deck.

"It's taken me many years to learn the secrets of magic that I know, but some people are just natural magicians," the performer says. "This will be a test to see if you have any hidden magical abilities that even you don't know about yet."

The magician smiles and continues, saying, "We will do this trick together, and I want you to do everything with your deck that I do with mine."

Having said this, the magician shuffles his deck and instructs the spectator to do likewise with his. Then they trade decks, and each selects a card from the deck he now holds. They each memorize their cards, and then each places his card on top of his deck. The decks are cut three times. Then the magician and spectator trade decks once again.

"Now I have your deck and you have mine," says the magician. "I will search through your deck to find your card, and I want you to search through my deck to find mine. But we should do this in a very special way. I'm going to find the card in your deck that is the same as the card I selected in my deck. And I want you to find the card in my deck that is the same as the one you picked from your deck."

When this is done, both people place their cards face down on the table. At the count of three, they both flip over their cards and, by magic, both cards are the same.

In this case, if the spectator asks you, "How did you do that?" you can turn around and ask him, "How did *you* do that?"

The secret: For this trick, you will need two decks of cards. If you do this trick with borrowed cards (preferable), any two standard decks will do. If you are performing this trick with your own cards, use pet decks: two decks of the same back design, a red-backed and a blue-backed deck.

One of the nice things about this trick is that it can be done at any time with any two decks without any pre-arrangement of the decks.

Begin by having the spectator select a deck. You take the other one, and you each shuffle your deck. In the process of shuffling, glance at and remember the bottom card in your deck. The two of you switch decks. The spectator now holds a deck with a bottom card that you know. Let's say it's the ace of spades. He picks a card from his deck, and you pick one from yours. It doesn't matter which card you pick since you need not remember it anyway. But pretend to be very particular and concerned about the card you choose. You put your card on top of your deck, and the spectator puts his on the top of his deck. Now you each cut your deck. This puts the spectator's card just under the ace of spades. You each cut your deck two more times. No matter how many times he cuts his deck, his chosen card will always be the one just beneath the ace of spades. (If, by any chance, the ace of spades should end up as the bottom card, then the spectator's card will be on top of the deck.)

You and the spectator switch decks; he tries to find your card while you try to find his. You tell him to look for the card identical to his, and that you will look for the card the same as yours. You simply find the card beneath the ace of spades and put it face down on the table. He finds the card identical to his and puts it face down on the table. When the cards are turned over, they will, of course, be the same card.

PART III

SPECIAL SKILLS

To become more than just a mechanical performer of complicated manual maneuvers, the magician must develop some skills of personal showmanship.

Chapter Seven describes some ways to develop your own patter, to illuminate your magic with the wonders of imagination.

In Chapter Eight, the practice of turning magic tricks into dramatic skits is discussed as an alternative to the more segmented magic show.

PATTER

G RAVELY, a magician approaches center stage, carefully holding a small box in her hand. She opens the box and says: "In this small box is nestled a sacred stone known as the 'Moonstone.' It first appeared in the days of King Arthur and the Knights of the Round Table. This is the stone of Merlin, the great magician, and there are some who say it was fashioned from the heart of a brave knight. It's been passed along over the years, from wizard to wizard, magician to magician. A few years ago, while I was traveling through England, the Moonstone came accidentally and unexpectedly into my possession, and here it is."

Simply by using language cleverly, the magician has converted an ordinary rock—which she may have found in her backyard garden—into a precious, enchanted charm. The words a magician uses while performing a trick are known as "patter." Patter can be a magician's staunchest ally in creating an illusion. A simple trick involving ordinary objects can take on a whole new dimension when fascinating patter is added. Sometimes, if the patter is tricky enough, it can nearly accomplish the trick for the performer.

To emphasize the uses of patter, let's take a simple but effective trick and consider several ways it might be performed.

The effect: The magician takes three different-colored cards—a red one, a blue one, and a yellow one—and places them in a hat. She removes the red one and the blue one. It turns out that the blue one is still in the hat, and the red and yellow cards have been removed.

The trick and secret: To do this trick, you will need *four* cards. Each can be made of cardboard and should be about the size of a standard playing card. One card is painted red on both sides, one is painted yellow on both sides, one is painted blue on both sides, and the fourth card—the gimmick—is painted blue on one side and yellow on the other side.

Before the trick, put the yellow card in your inside coat pocket. When the trick starts, hold the other cards so that the audience sees either side of the red card, either side of the blue card, and the yellow side of the yellow/blue gimmicked card. In full view, drop the three cards into an empty hat. Withdraw the gimmick showing only the *blue* side and put it in your inside coat pocket. The audience will think you have withdrawn the blue card, but it is still in the hat. Next, take the red card from the hat. You can be a bit more casual here, since it doesn't matter which side you show with this card. Put the red card in your inside coat pocket.

The audience now thinks that the yellow card remains in the hat, but actually a blue card remains there. Turn the hat upside down, and the blue card will drop out, to the amazement of the audience. As smoothly as possible, withdraw the red and yellow cards from your pocket, leaving the gimmicked card hidden there.

At this point, the three regular cards and even the hat can be passed out for examination by the audience.

The three colors used in this illusion lend themselves to the creation of stories which can be converted into patter. The patter might go something like this:

THE FRUIT SALAD. "I'm not a very good cook," the magician says, "but I do make a pretty good fruit salad. The secret of my fruit salad is that I use the freshest apples, the firmest blueberries, and the tastiest bananas."

So saying, the magician displays the red card for apples, the blue card for blueberries, and the yellow card for bananas.

"I cut them up and place them in a bowl, and everyone loves them." As she says this, the magician places the cards in the hat.

"Well, almost everyone. As you might expect, there is one problem eater in my family. I guess every family has one. It's my Uncle Wilbur. Oh, he eats the blueberries. In fact, he likes blueberries better than any other fruit." The magician takes the gimmicked card, displaying the blue side, and puts it in her pocket.

"In fact, although he's not crazy about apples, he even eats the apples." The magician takes the red card from the hat and places it in her pocket.

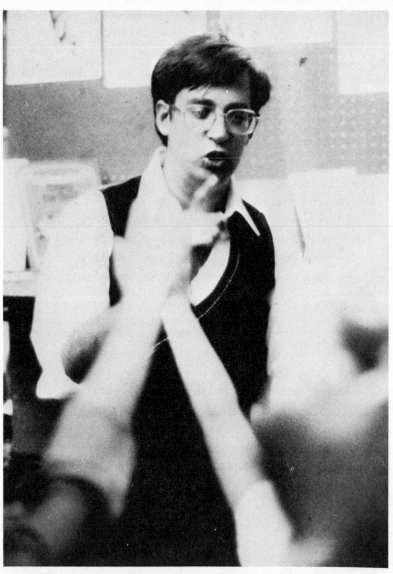

Author Jay Boyar tries out some new patter in his magic act during a street fair in mid-Manhattan. (JANE KRUPP)

"But he absolutely refuses to eat the bananas. So what I always do is, after I dish out the fruit salad to everyone except Uncle Wilbur, I make a magic pass over the serving bowl and change the bananas into blueberries." The magician tips the hat upside down and the blue card falls out.

"And the strangest thing about it is that I use exactly the same amount of blueberries, apples, and bananas." The magician, in saying this, takes the red and yellow cards from her pocket and places them with the blue card.

That's a good way to do the trick, and it gives the audience a vivid picture to imagine, rather than just three cards to look at. If you are a convincing speaker, it almost seems like you've done the trick with actual fruit.

There are many, many other ways that the trick can be done. Using the same procedure, several other patter illusions can be created.

THE BIRDS. "I love birds. They make wonderful pets because of their lovely music and their striking colors. Not long ago, I went to a pet store where there were three birds: a red one (a cardinal), a blue one (a blue jay), and a yellow one (a canary). I had a hard time deciding which bird to buy, but I finally bought the blue jay and brought it home," says the magician.

"It was lovely, so the next day I went back to the pet store and I got the red one and brought it home, too," she continues.

"Then I got to thinking that the yellow bird must be very lonely sitting in that pet store all by itself. So I went back to buy it, but the strangest thing happened. When I got there, the yellow bird was gone and there was only a blue bird that looked and sounded incredibly like the blue jay I had already bought. I bought this other blue bird and brought it home.

"But when I got there, I was surprised to find that what I had was a cardinal, a blue jay, and a canary."

Another variation would be to do the trick as before, substituting the color blue for the color yellow and vice versa. Then you could tell the following story:

THE TWINS. "Once upon a time there was a set of twins, a boy and a girl. They had been born on December 14 (or whatever day it happens to be when you perform the trick). Every year, their parents bought them identical gifts.

"One year, they both wanted hats. The boy wanted a blue hat, and the girl wanted a red one. Their mother went to a girl's clothing store and brought home a red hat. Their father went to a boy's clothing store and tried to get a blue hat. But the salesclerk, whose name was Sammy and who was new at the store, made a mistake and wrapped up a yellow hat. Unknowingly, the father brought home the yellow hat. A little later that day, Sammy realized his mistake when he saw the blue hat still in the store. But luckily, Sammy was something of an amateur magician, too. He made a magic pass, and the blue hat turned yellow. Back at home, the boy's hat which had been yellow turned blue. So both of the twins, who had been very good that year, got the hats they wanted and had happy birthdays."

There you have three very different ways of doing the same trick, and there are countless others. These are just

examples. The best way to do a magic trick, and that
includes all the tricks in this book, is to devise your own
method of presentation. If you choose to tell a story, then
make up your own story based on your personality and
the trick in question.

Sometimes patter can be used to accomplish almost the
entire trick. Care in phrasing can turn what sounds like
ordinary speech into sneaky sentences with trap doors and
hidden springs which confound the spectators, leaving
them quite baffled. The illusion described below is an
example of just such a trick.

MIND OVER MATTER

The effect: A spectator seems to name one card at random. The magician then produces a pack of playing cards,
and the spectator tells the magician what position in the
deck he would like his card to be in. The selected card is
found to be in that very position in the deck!

The trick and secret: Before starting the trick, the magician takes a deck of cards and picks one picture card at
random out of sight of the audience. Let us suppose it is
the jack of diamonds. He places this card on top of the
deck, puts the cards in a packet, and puts the packet out
of sight in his pocket. Then the trick begins.

"Sometimes, when the wind is right and all the cosmic
currents are flowing properly, I can perform feats of
mentalism that could astound Svengali. Let me see . . ."
the magician says, wetting his forefinger and holding it in

Young magician Sam Chamberlain invents a tall tale to tell while performing some impromptu card tricks for a friend.

the air. "Yes . . . yes . . . I think we can do something rather astounding tonight, if everyone concentrates very hard.

"Now, there are four suits in the deck: hearts, diamonds, spades, and clubs." Choosing a spectator at random, the magician asks him to *name* two of those suits. That is the secret to the trick. The magician says "name" two suits, not "pick" or "choose," but "name." That could mean anything. Since the card selected beforehand is the jack of diamonds, the spectator must be forced into selecting diamonds. If one of the suits the spectator names is diamonds (suppose he names diamonds and hearts), the magician just smiles and repeats those words: "Diamonds and hearts."

But if the spectator should select two suits, neither of which is diamonds (suppose clubs and spades are chosen), then the magician just smiles and says, "That leaves diamonds and hearts."

In either case, through tricky wording, we now have diamonds and hearts. The magician then says, "Would you name one of them, please?" to another spectator. If the spectator says, "Diamonds," the magician, like before, simply repeats it. If the spectator says, "Hearts," then the magician simply says, "Which leaves us with diamonds." In either case, the suit diamonds has been forced.

Next, the magician says, "There are two kinds of cards in the suit of diamonds, picture cards and number cards." He points to another spectator and asks, "Would you please name either pictures or numbers? In the same manner as before, the magician forces "pictures."

"There are three picture cards in the suit of diamonds," the magician continues. "King, queen, and jack. Would you please name two of those." Still another spectator names two cards. If she names king and queen, the magician says, "That leaves us with the jack. The jack of diamonds." If the spectator picks jack and king, the magician says, "Fine. Now would you name one of those?" At this point, if the jack is named, the magician just says, "The jack of diamonds." If the king is named, the magician says, "That leaves us with the jack. The jack of diamonds." The magician does basically the same thing if the spectator says "jack and queen," substituting "queen" for "king" in the patter.

In effect, the jack of diamonds has been forced. At this point, the magician asks the spectator to name any number from 1 to 52. Suppose the spectator names 25. The magician takes the deck from his pocket and holds it in his hand (face down) and counts off the first card (the jack of diamonds) face down onto the table. As he does this he says, "One." He continues counting, placing each successive card on top of the one before it until he reaches 25. Then he flips the whole pile of 25 cards over and shows the jack of diamonds. The spectator will think it was the twenty-fifth card when actually it was the first. This will, of course, work no matter what number the spectator selects.

This trick may seem very simple to detect, but actually —if you use your patter smoothly—it will fool them every time.

CHAPTER EIGHT

MAGIC AS THEATER

WHEN a play called *The Magic Show* opened on Broadway in New York City, it was a breakthrough in the world of magic. For the first time on a large scale, a magic performance was presented in the context of a play. Doug Henning, the magician at the center of the show, played the role of a magician in a show that was, really, a "backstage musical" with magic.

A "backstage musical" is a musical play about putting on a musical play. *The Magic Show* was a musical magic show in the form of a play about putting on a magic show.

This production was different from most magic performances in that the play which surrounded the illusions was actually a play, in the traditional sense of the word. There were several actors, each of whom played a different character. There was a specific plot that strung the tricks —and the songs—together.

All of the dialogue had been written down and rehearsed until the actors remembered it exactly. This is quite different from a typical magic show, in which the conjurer has a good general idea of what he will say but leaves a certain amount of room for improvisation and the accidental, spontaneous occurrences that so often happen in the course of a magic show.

In *The Magic Show*, the characters talked to each other, not to the audience as they do in most magic performances. Most people very much enjoyed either the plot or the songs or, most often, the magic tricks themselves, or even all of these elements.

When anything is as successful as that, it is likely to inspire imitation. In this case, I hope that's true. Not that I'd like to see magicians all over America copying the tricks, plot, and tunes of "the Magic Show." Rather, the concept of theater linked with magic is one that ought to be developed more. Using magic as a part of a more elaborate play has possibilities that have as yet hardly been tapped.

Putting on a magical play, as opposed to a magic show, has special problems of its own. The practical problems involved in accomplishing this feat can be more difficult to resolve than those encountered in making an elephant vanish!

Perhaps the biggest problem is that of people. A magic show can be presented with only the magician (and perhaps an assistant or two) performing on stage. But for a play to work, it is almost always necessary for there to be several actors, all of whom must be available for each performance.

Another problem is space. Most magic shows are developed so that they can be performed from place to place, with some flexibility. A living room, a basement, a garage, a den—any of these might serve as the magician's stage. Generally, a magician does only a show or two in any given place. Then he is on the move (see Chapter Nine).

For a young magician trying to stage a play, just finding a space to perform it can be a big problem. You will probably want to perform the play at least several times, so a space that will be available for several performances must be obtained, and it's best if the same space is used for the run of the show.

Not only that, but you will have to have rehearsals somewhere, and it's always best to rehearse in the same room in which you intend to perform.

When you're starting out, your best bet might be to use your family's or a neighbor's garage or basement, providing one is available when you need it.

You might be able to interest someone at your school in your show. A drama or English teacher, perhaps, might be willing to help you arrange to use a room (or stage) in the school. Maybe your teacher will even be interested in helping to prepare the production in other ways.

Assuming you work out all the practical and technical problems in presenting a magic play (and they can be overcome, by the way, with a little persistence), you will then have the problem of finding a magic play to perform. There just aren't very many of these to choose from.

I suggest that you write your own, either alone or with a friend. Make copies of the play and give one to each cast member.

Printed here is a one-act play for two actors that I've

written to give you an idea of the sort of thing you can do. I have used some of the tricks described elsewhere in this book and woven them into a play. This play is *not* included here to encourage anyone to perform it, but rather to give you an understanding of how magic and theater can be blended.

JUST WHISTLE

> SCENE: *We are in a young boy's or girl's room. It could be either, but, just to choose one, let's say it's a girl's room. There is a table and a chair, and the walls are decorated with pictures of movie stars and sports heroes and rock stars. In the middle of the room, the girl, Marilyn, stands, blowing air through her lips, a pained expression on her face. She gets discouraged, sits down on the chair, and puts her head on the table. Perhaps she is crying. Mysterious music begins, and Marilyn lifts her head, wondering about its source. A wizard enters dramatically. He wears a cone-shaped hat and a long, flowing robe and has a lengthy silver gray beard. In his hand, he carries a wand.*

MARILYN (startled): Wh-who are you?

WIZARD: (He whistles.) I'm a wizard. (He whistles again.) The Whistling Wizard, to be exact. Why are you crying?

MARILYN: I wasn't crying!

WIZARD: Well, you weren't exactly laughing, either. Now, were you?

MARILYN: No. I guess not.

WIZARD: Why are you so sad, Marilyn?

MARILYN: Well, I'm trying to learn how to whistle, and it's just so hard!

WIZARD: I thought so.

MARILYN: Everyone in my class at school can whistle except me. I've been trying to learn for weeks, and I just can't seem to get the hang of it. It's too hard. It's impossible!

WIZARD: Now Marilyn. There are many things in the world that may be impossible, but whistling just isn't one of them.

MARILYN: You're wrong. It's impossible!

WIZARD: Marilyn, have you got a ring?

MARILYN: Sure. (She shows it to him on her finger.)

WIZARD: Lend it to me for a moment. (She removes the ring and hands it to the Wizard. He places it over his wand.) Now, what would you say if I said I could make this ring float?

MARILYN: Impossible.

WIZARD: Well, watch. (To audience) When I say "three," help me out by whistling. Ready? One, two three! (Wizard and the audience whistle, and the ring floats up and down on the wand until finally the ring pops off. The Wizard returns the ring to Marilyn, and she puts it on her finger. The secret to this trick is found in Chapter Five.)

MARILYN: Gosh! That was amazing!

WIZARD: You said that it was impossible, a minute ago.

MARILYN: I guess I did.

WIZARD: And how do you feel about whistling now?

MARILYN: Still impossible. (She tries to whistle and fails.)

WIZARD: Now, Marilyn, is there a hat in this room?

MARILYN: Right here.

WIZARD: You see that it's empty. (He shows it to her and the audience.)

MARILYN: Yes.

WIZARD: Now observe these three cards. This red one is an apple, the blue one is a blueberry, and the yellow one is a banana. I drop them into the hat. First, I'll take out the blueberry, then I'll take out the apple. (He does so and puts them into a pocket in his robe.) What is left?

MARILYN: The banana, of course.

WIZARD: And what if I tell you that you're wrong?

MARILYN: That's impossible.

WIZARD: Really? One, two, three! (Wizard and the audience whistle.) Reach into the hat and take out the last card. (She does so, and it's the blue one. The Wizard reaches into his pocket and pulls out the red and yellow cards. The hat is shown to be empty. The secret to this trick is found in Chapter Seven.)

MARILYN: That's incredible!

WIZARD: A moment ago you said it was impossible.

MARILYN: I guess I did.

WIZARD: And how do you feel about whistling, now?

MARILYN: Impossible!

WIZARD: Hmm . . . Marilyn, have you got any ink?

MARILYN: Sure. Right here. (She shows him a glass of black ink on the table.)

WIZARD: Stir it up a little, will you? (She takes a stick, stirs the ink, and then wipes the stick off. The Wizard picks up the glass of ink and covers it with a cloth.) Now, Marilyn, what would you say if I told you that I was going to change the ink to water?

MARILYN: I'd have to say that that's impossible.

WIZARD: Okay, watch! One, two, three! (The Wizard and the audience whistle. He removes the cloth from the glass, and the glass is now seen to be full of water. The secret to this trick is found in Chapter Twelve.)

MARILYN: That's astounding!

WIZARD: But not impossible.

MARILYN: No.

WIZARD: And what about whistling?

MARILYN: Still impossible.

WIZARD: Hmmm . . . Look, Marilyn, I've got to go. But before I do, let me tell you that that glass isn't full of just ordinary water. That's Whistling Water. (The mysterious music starts again.) Oh-oh. I've really got to be on my way. But remember what I said. Goodbye, Marilyn. (Wizard exits.)

MARILYN: Goodbye. (She walks over to the glass and looks at it.) Whistling Water? (She listens to it but hears nothing.) Whistling Water? (She takes a sip and tries to whistle, but fails. She shakes her head. She sits on the chair for a moment, then walks around to the glass and takes another sip. She tries to whistle and then fails again. She shakes her head. She puts the hat on her head, looks at the ring on her finger, and goes over to the glass again, taking another sip.) One, two, three! (She whistles!)

Curtain.

PART IV

SETTING THE STAGE

On stage the magician must be surrounded by a magical atmosphere. The following two chapters deal with the atmosphere of a magic show and describe how to go about creating the setting that is most appropriate for the specific type of program you have in mind.

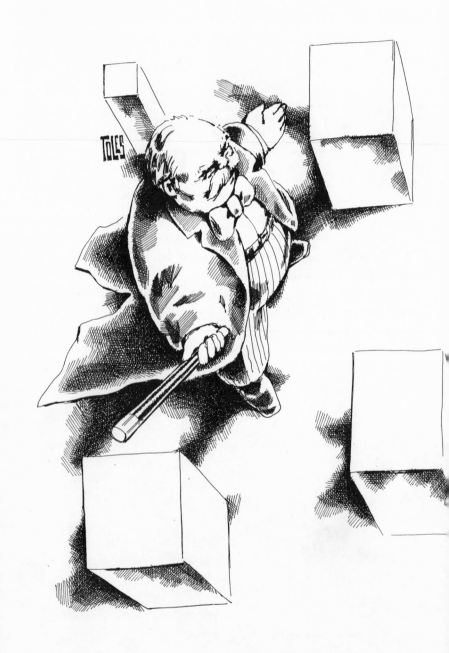

CHAPTER NINE

STAGE SPACES

ONCE upon a time, magic halls existed. These were theaters where, each evening, a magic show was presented. These halls were especially adapted for magicians and magic tricks. Sometimes, a particular magician was good enough (or lucky enough) to be the featured performer for years and years in a magic hall. He would get to know the stage very well, and he'd know exactly what kinds of effects were the most possible —and most successful—in that hall.

Today, this practice survives in a much diminished form. An establishment called The Magic Castle features mostly magic acts and is located in Hollywood. The Magic Town House, in New York City, has much the same atmosphere.

For the most part, however, the practice of maintaining magic halls has fallen away today. Magicians tend to travel around a lot, performing in whatever settings they can find: high school auditoriums, lodge halls, gymnasiums, on the street, and in private homes. This has, in a way, always been the magician's lot. Like most actors and entertainers throughout history, he has usually had to be a gypsy. In the days of vaudeville, most magicians—like singers and jugglers and comedians—traveled from town to town, bringing their act to a new audience every day of the week.

Today the young performer designing his act for the first time is well advised to take into account that at the start of his career his show will generally be performed at parties in private living rooms, family rooms, and basements. These are spaces that are not designed for a theatrical performance but rather for gatherings of friends and family. Many times the magician will never have seen the place in which he's performing until just a few minutes before his act goes on. And often, the magician himself will have to personally haul all of his magical equipment from his own home to each of the places where he'll be performing his magic.

Certain limitations present themselves because of this. For one thing, it's important to have an act that you can set up fairly quickly. Some giant tricks demand weeks of preparation with an army of assistants. In your own private theater you can take all day setting up your show. But when you're performing in someone's living room, you have to be able to set up quickly, and generally, you must work alone or with one assistant.

I have found that 30–45 minutes is really all the time your act should take to set up. When it is over, it should take no more than 15–20 minutes to pack and tidy up. Remember, the space in which you will be performing may have some other use scheduled for it just before or after you do your own show. It's a good idea to practice and time how long it takes to set up and take down a show, just as you might practice and time the show itself.

If you live in a big city, perhaps you will get to the site of your magic show by bus or subway. In this case, you'll have to drastically limit what you carry so that it is adaptable to public transportation. Perhaps only two medium-sized suitcases are all you'd be able to carry from show to show.

But let's assume that you get to the site of your shows by automobile and that you have the car's trunk and, per-

Magician Judi Lynn Zollweg gets some pointers in silk handkerchief magic from magic dealer Bob Little.

haps, a back seat in which to load your equipment. You still won't be able to perform the vanishing elephant trick, but a lot more possibilities will open up for you.

Upon arriving at the house where you are to perform your show, take a moment to look around at all the possible places to perform. Most homes have several rooms that are suitable for a magic show. You will want to select the best of the possibilities.

It's always desirable to do your show in a room in which nothing else is going on that day. If you're performing at a birthday party and the kids are playing pin-the-tail-on-the-donkey in the family room and if they are going to have cake and ice cream in the basement, then perhaps the living room would be best for the magic show. While it's not absolutely necessary, privacy is very desirable in setting up and taking down your show so that no secrets are accidentally revealed.

It's a good idea to select a room that allows you to set up with your back to a wall. Many times a trick will be designed so that from the front a secret is hidden, but from the back it is revealed. For that reason, you don't want people walking behind you as you're performing. A wall—not a window (unless it has opaque drapes)—to your back will solve this problem.

It's also best if the audience has comfortable seating during the show. Chairs aren't always necessary or even desirable. A carpeted floor often makes the best seating for an audience of children. There should be adequate lighting. At the very least, you should have the kind of standard lighting found in the rooms of most homes. However, if it is possible, you can illuminate the stage area and keep the audience area in darkness for a dramatic touch. Light should always shine on the front of the set and the performer, never from the back and into the eyes of the audience.

If you use any electrical aids—like recorded music, for example—you should be certain that there is an electrical outlet nearby in the room.

If you're performing in someone's home and there are valuable or delicate objects in the room, you might want to place them somewhere else until the show is over. Even if you don't knock them over, someone in the audience might. You also should be aware that if any of your tricks involve animals or water or are messy in any way, you should take this into account when choosing a room. You are, after all, a guest in someone's home.

How you choose to set the stage in your act will depend to a great extent on what tricks you'll be performing. Your setup should be considered in terms of the specific magic tricks you are doing. However, a good general rule is to get some movement into your show by performing different tricks from different locations on stage.

Many magicians use a setup like the one pictured in Figure A. Tables 1 and 2 are small, portable T.V. tables. Table 1 is stage left (to the performer's left), and Table 2 is stage right. If the audience is to be seated on the floor (and especially if it's composed mostly of children), it's a good idea to set these tables a foot or two closer to the audience than you would consider ideal. The kids will usually crowd up close to the tables as they sit down.

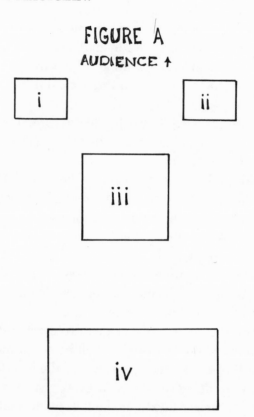

FIGURE A
AUDIENCE ↑

Then, just before you begin your act, move those tables back a foot or two and you'll have a couple of feet between you and your audience, which makes for better sight lines and more ease in performing.

Table 3 is generally a firmer, more substantial table (like a folding card table), but a T.V. table might be used here, too. It's a good idea to cover all these tables in matching cloths. It will give your setup a unified, impressive look, and it helps conceal the fact that the tables are so flimsy.

Table 4 can be any kind of large table. This is the table where you place anything you don't immediately need. It is a worktable. You can consider it "backstage," and you should not draw attention to it by putting a colorful cloth on it. It is a good idea to have a box of some kind on this table in case you have to quickly dispose of a tricky prop so that it is hidden from the audience. You might be able to save yourself some difficulty by borrowing this table from the people who own the place where you are performing. Since almost any large table will do for Table 4, you need not carry a special one around with you. However, if you intend to borrow this table when you get to the site of your performance, be sure to phone ahead to ask permission to use it.

It's often a good idea to begin a trick at one table, continue to another, and end at a third. This gives a certain sweep and motion to your act. You may notice that an air of informality and intimacy is more possible at the smaller tables than at Table 3. If you have some little, humorous tricks you might want to set them on Tables 1 and 2. If you have an austere, mysterious illusion, Table 3 might be best for it.

It is important to realize that the visual impact of your setup often sets the tone for your entire show. It should reflect your style. If you do a lot of oriental-type tricks, for instance, you might want to use elements of oriental design and calligraphy in your stage setup. If your act is mostly humorous, a humorous-looking set will be in order. It's important that the set be eye-catching and colorful, although even this rule can be broken if your act is of a certain type. The best thing to do is to think about your act, your tricks, and your personality, and then set out to design a set that reflects the most important elements of all three.

THREE-RING CIRCUS

The effect: The magician shows three paper rings, cuts each one down the center, and emerges with three different results.

The trick: The magician begins center stage, in front of Table 3, between Tables 1 and 2. "Once upon a time," he says, "there was a great circus that toured throughout Europe. It was a three-ring circus, and it featured lions, tigers, elephants, trapeze artists, clowns, jugglers, wire walkers, sword swallowers, fire-eaters, and one wonderful magician. One day, for lunch, the circus cook served some rotten soup by mistake, and everyone in the circus had a bellyache and had to stay in bed that night. The only person who felt fine was the magician, who, instead of soup, had made himself some rabbit stew that afternoon. He decided to put on a show by himself that night, because, after all, the show must go on. Since a three-ring circus had been advertised, this is the trick he did."

The magician walks over to Table 1, where a large ring of paper is resting. "This is the first ring," he says, as he starts to cut the ring down the center, all the way around.

"Now, if I cut a ring down the center, when I reach the end what should I be left with?" The correct answer, of course, is "two rings." And when someone in the audience guesses it, the magician tells her she's correct. As a matter of fact, she *is* correct; the magician does end up with two rings, both of which he gives to audience members as souvenirs.

The magician then moves to Table 2 on which is a ring that looks identical to the ring that was on Table 1. He begins to cut it and explains to the audience that this should yield the same results. Just before he makes the final cut, he makes a pass over the ring. "You see," he says, "we have two rings, but they are *magically linked together*." He gives the linked rings to someone in the audience.

Finally, the magician steps over to Table 3 and takes from it a third, identical-looking ring. As he cuts it, he reminds the audience of the two previous results. Just before making the final cut, he makes a magic pass over the ring. This time, instead of two rings, the magician has one giant ring, which he gives to an audience member.

The secret: This trick works itself if you do just a little bit of advance preparation.

You will need three rings, each of which is made from a strip of paper 2″ wide × 44″ long. (Shelf paper is often a good choice to start with in making your rings. Just cut off a piece 44″ long, and cut that into strips 2″ wide. Then glue, paste, or tape the beginning of each strip to its end.) The trick is that while the first ring is a nice, smooth one, the second ring is made by twisting the strip once before

FIGURE B

FIGURE C

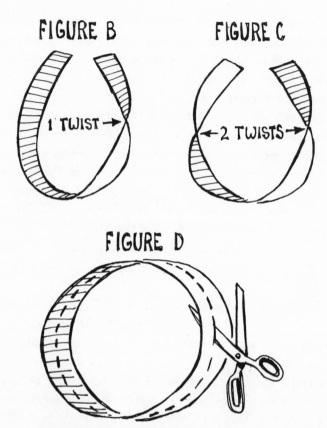

FIGURE D

gluing it (Figure B), and the third is made by twisting it twice before gluing (Figure C). The audience won't notice these twists. Then just cut down the center (Figure D) of each ring in turn, and the trick works exactly as described.

Variation I: Rings of varying colors are sometimes used, although many magicians swear that the one-color effect is best.

Variation II: Another possibility is to begin with one thick ring, made the following way. Take a large ring—made with a 4″ x 44″ strip of paper—and just before gluing one end to the other, cut one end down the center, about 5 or 6″ (Figure E).

Twist Tab X once before gluing and Tab Y twice. After you cut the ring down the middle in front of the audience, you will have two rings. Cut the ring with Tab X, and you'll get two linked rings. Cut the ring with Tab Y, and you'll get one large ring.

FIGURE E

1 TWIST →   ← 2 TWISTS

CHAPTER TEN

MAGIC WITH MUSIC

MAGIC and music go together like peanut butter and jelly. A room filled with music is a room transformed. The type of music that's heard sets the tone for the people watching the show.

When magic was in its heyday, a magician frequently performed on a bill with an orchestra. For part of the show, the magician would perform alone. Other parts would have the magician and the musicians performing together. Still other parts would have the musicians performing by themselves. It would be, in effect, an evening of magic and music.

When the great escape artist Harry Houdini performed, he frequently used music in a very special way. He would be bound up in some escape-proof contraption (such as handcuffs, a straitjacket, or a wooden box nailed shut), and then he'd be surrounded by a curtain so that no one could see how he was attempting to escape.

While he was hidden from view, the orchestra would

105

play and the audience—anxious about Houdini—would become increasingly agitated. Sometimes Houdini would be trapped in a dangerous situation (underwater, perhaps), and the audience would actually become fearful that he was running out of air and close to death. The joke was that, more times than not, Houdini would already have escaped and was just waiting behind the curtain, perfectly free and safe, while the orchestra played on until the audience reached a fever pitch. Then he'd emerge unharmed. Now *that* was showmanship.

These days, few magicians are escape artists and even fewer find themselves in positions where they are fortunate enough to work with an orchestra. The music most magicians use is prerecorded, and in fact, this is especially true of young magicians, who are likely to be performing in private homes and small restaurants.

Probably the best way to use recorded music is to put it on a portable cassette and use a cassette player. The sound quality of a compact cassette player is usually better than that of a compact turntable record player, and a machine that is small and easy to set up is a very valuable asset for the traveling magician. I strongly advise against borrowing a tape recorder, cassette player, or record player from the people who are hiring you. It's too easy to break someone else's machine or have something go wrong.

If you are performing in a big hall, you will probably be provided with a microphone. If there is no way to electronically patch or channel your music through the sound system, a good trick is to put the microphone (when you are not speaking into it) next to your cassette player and let the music travel through the sound system in that way.

Investing in a cassette tape player is a good idea for a magician who is starting out. Not only does music add a whole new dimension to your show, but the cassette player (if it can record, too) can be used for a variety of other things. You can tape-record yourself performing a trick and then play the tape back for yourself, listening to hear how smoothly—or awkwardly—you speak while performing.

Whatever kind of music reproduction system you have (and if you don't have one, you could save up for one with the money you earn performing), there are all kinds of ways to use music. You can use it to play in the background as you are being introduced and as you make your entrance at the start of your show. You can pantomime a trick and have specially selected music playing in the background as you perform.

The main point to remember is that music is a very powerful force. You will want to consider very carefully what a specific piece of music does to the overall mood of the trick and the *entire show* before you incorporate it into your act.

If you want a bright, fast tune, you could use a favorite pop tune of yours that you might have heard on the radio. Or, if a trick seems to call for a dark, mysterious sound, something like Saint-Saens's "Danse Macabre" might work best.

As you go through a typical day, listen closely to the

In Oriental attire, Dr. Chang (Russell Glover) combines magic and music. The odd instrument he holds is a cross between a clarinet and a plumber's helper!

music that you hear. If you hear a tune that seems to you to fit a trick you plan on performing, see if you can get a recording of the music for your show. Be aware of the various kinds of music that there are and how these different sounds affect your own mood.

One final note on music. It's important that the music be compatible with the trick that you perform with it, or it may actually distract the audience from the magic rather than intensify the experience. For this reason, I almost never use music with people singing lyrics, because the audience tends to listen to the lyrics rather than watch the trick closely. Also, I avoid music that is closely identified in the minds of the audience with some other presentation like a television commercial or program or a popular movie.

THIRSTY

The effect: The magician produces a glass of milk from nowhere.

The trick: Music starts, and it is a strange, mysterious melody like "Danse Macabre." The magician displays two tubes to the audience, one nestled inside the other. The inside tube is bright orange, the outer tube is jet black and has a window cut out of the front of it which allows the audience to see the orange tube inside.

The magician picks up the black tube and silently shows it to the audience, moving in time with the music. She looks through it at the spectators and moves it back and forth so that the entire audience gets a good look. The magician might even take her wand and rotate it inside the tube.

She then places the black tube back over the orange one and lifts the orange one up and repeats the same movements, showing it to the audience. She then puts the orange tube back in its place inside the black tube.

Both sides of a black opaque cloth are shown to the audience and placed over the tubes. The magician waves her wand over the top of this and removes the cloth. With one hand, the magician removes the black tube, holding it up so that the audience can see that it is empty. Then, with the other hand, the magician removes the orange tube and holds it so that the audience can see inside. Resting on the table, where the tubes were, is a nice fresh glass of milk. As the applause starts and the music fades out, the magician takes a sip of milk and, perhaps, pours it into another container to demonstrate that it is really milk.

The secret: To do this trick, you will need two tubes: One is about 7″ tall and 4″ in diameter, while the other tube is slightly shorter and narrower so that it fits easily inside the larger one. You may have to hunt around a little for tubes that work. The supermarket and the hardware store are good places to start hunting.

Cut a square window in the larger tube so that it is centrally located with about 2″ on each side (Figure A).

Find a glass that fits easily into the smaller tube. Get a piece of very black, thick cloth, and make a sleeve that fits around the glass. It should be about ½″ taller than

FIGURE A

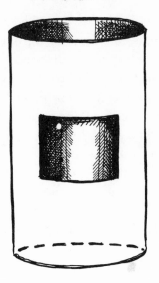

the glass. The sleeve should be tight enough around the glass so that it won't slip down, but loose enough so that it is easily and smoothly pulled off the glass.

Put the glass in the cloth sleeve, put the sleeve in the small tube, and put the small tube inside the big tube. Place all this on a table. It's best if there is a black cloth on the table.

The audience will see this as simply two tubes, one inside the other. When you remove the outer, black tube, the audience will see just the inner, orange tube. When you replace the black tube and remove the orange tube, the black tube will appear to be empty because the audience will see nothing but the black cloth sleeve through the black tube's window, and to an audience that will look like a dark empty space.

Proceed with the trick as described above. When you remove the opaque cloth from the top of the tubes, secretly grab the cloth sleeve, too, and casually place both the opaque cloth and the hidden cloth sleeve out of sight of the audience, on a rear table or behind a prop. You will be left with two tubes covering a glass of milk. When the time comes to remove both tubes, the audience will be amazed to find a fresh glass of milk.

Note: Many novelty and magic shops sell liquids and tablets (which cost only a few cents each) which, when mixed with a glass of water, create a liquid that looks very much like milk. Many magicians prefer to use this because it is easier to transport, never goes sour, and is cheaper than milk. One drawback to these liquids and tablets is that you should not sip this stuff, so the audience may not as fully believe that it is milk. However, if, at the end of the trick, you pour the liquid into another container (like a pitcher), the audience will be convinced that it is a liquid.

PART

V BEHIND
THE SCENES

In magic, what the audience doesn't know about or doesn't see is usually the most important part of the performer's job.

Secrets and practice, two ideas of paramount concern to the magician, are discussed in Chapters Eleven and Twelve. In Chapter Thirteen, the relationship of the assistant to the magician is explained.

Then, in Chapter Fourteen, the relationship of magicians to each other is illustrated by the events of an international convention of magicians.

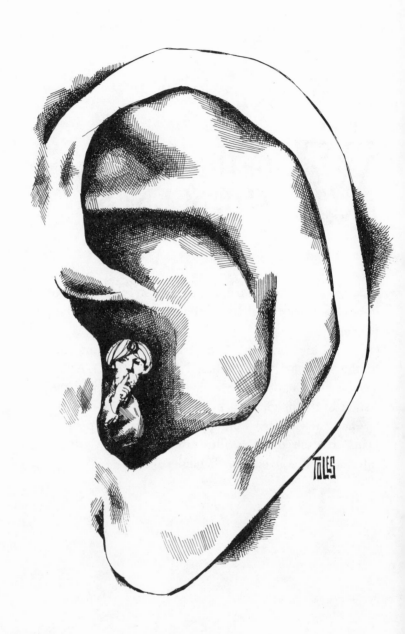

CHAPTER ELEVEN

SECRETS

ALL professions have their secrets, called trade secrets. For the magician, trade secrets assume added importance.

What separates the magician from most other performers is that this job involves fooling people with secret methods. There is no escaping the fact that no matter how entertaining, charming, and engaging a magician might be, it isn't worth a thing unless he or she is also able to fool the audience. Quite naturally, then, magicians are very careful about guarding their secrets.

When you are starting out as a magician, it is often rather hard to keep your secrets to yourself. After performing an astounding illusion, you begin to hear the pleas of your audience to divulge the secret of the trick. You want to be an agreeable person, so you are tempted to reveal your secrets.

Don't. No matter how much spectators plead, they don't really want to know how the trick is done.

For one thing, most magic tricks have such simple solutions that typical spectators will be disappointed when they hear how a trick is done. They will have been imagining an intricate and mysterious solution, and when you reveal your elementary answer they will feel cheated. They may also feel a little stupid, too.

There is another reason why many spectators don't truly want to know the secrets to magic tricks. Even though our common sense tells us that there is a reasonable explanation to every magic trick, there is a part of each of us that wants to believe in the incredible, the supernatural. As long as the spectator is kept in the dark about how a trick is done, the possibility of the supernatural is kept alive. The moment you reveal the secret, that possibility perishes.

This is not to suggest that you should actually represent yourself as some kind of honest-to-goodness miracle worker. That would be fraud. But as long as you call yourself a magician—a conjurer—and as long as you make clear that what you are doing is just a show, then whatever you say in the course of that show is all part of the act. It would be as foolish for you to say, "By the way, what I did is just a trick," as it would be for an actor playing Hamlet to interrupt that play and explain, "By the way, I'm not really Hamlet. I'm just an actor dressed up and wearing makeup." That would shatter the illusion you're creating. There is plenty of time for saying such things after the show is packed up.

In fact, many magicians avoid the use of the word "trick" on stage because it implies that there is no real hocus-pocus involved. Instead, words like "feat" or "spectacle" or "illusion" are often substituted.

Remember: There are at least two good reasons to keep your secrets—(1) so that you can continue to perform the trick and fool audiences; and (2) because the audience itself doesn't really want to know the secrets.

If people badger you about how you do your tricks, it often helps to have some clever answers to put them off. When someone asks, "How did you do that?" you can assume an expression of confusion and say, "I don't know." Then smile, to confirm that you're not telling.

Another answer is to make up some bizarre story about mirrors or spirits or anything at all. The spectator will quickly figure out that you have no intention of giving a straight answer and will relent.

One answer that usually works when people ask, "How did you do that?" is to simply say, "Magic!" They will probably ask again, and all you need to do is repeat that same answer.

Perhaps the best answer is, "I promised not to tell." It doesn't matter whom you promise, people usually won't ask. But since you ought to promise someone, you can promise me. Simply sign the statement below:

I promise never to reveal the secrets of magic learned in this book (or elsewhere) to anyone at any time except:
1. To duly authorized magical assistants
2. To students wishing to become magicians
3. To other magicians
4. Through publications designed for magicians.

_____

(SIGNATURE)

It's a good idea to write out a similar statement and ask your assistants to sign it. In any case, all your assistants should be made aware that whatever magic they may learn from you is not to be revealed to anyone else.

Another comment that is often shouted from the audience—and this is especially true if the group includes a large number of children—is, "I know how to do that!"

Strangely, it doesn't seem to matter at what point in the trick you are: You may have finished, you may just be picking up a deck of cards to begin, or you may be anywhere along the line. Somehow, no magician can get very far in his or her act without hearing that cry.

As a matter of fact, the person who says it usually does not know how to do the trick at all. He may know how to do *a* trick, or he may know *one way* to do the trick you are performing, but chances are that he is just showing off.

In any case, one thing you might reply is, "So do I!" Often an unruly child can be cured if you just ignore him or, better yet, invite him up to be an assistant. That usually quiets him down.

Once in a while, I encounter a really noisy child at a performance. What I usually do is ask him to come on stage. Then, I hand him a small piece of rope that I have ready for just such occasions. I ask him to stand at the side of the stage, holding the rope tightly, and wait.

After a trick or two, I take the rope back, thank him, and ask him to return to his seat. This trick is usually enough to keep him quiet for the rest of the show.

It goes without saying that you, as a magician, should always be a good audience for other magicians. Since you are a magician, there is no need for you to ever show off by saying, "I know how that trick is done," or to badger the performer into telling you secrets.

As a matter of fact, most magicians are perfectly willing

to swap secrets with other magicians when the occasion presents itself (see Chapter Fourteen). Few magicians, however, are ready to tell other magicians everything they know.

IT'S IN THE BAG

The effect: A bag is shown empty, and an egg seems to vanish and reappear in the bag at will.

The trick: "Audiences so often want to know how a magician does her tricks, I always try to include one trick in each performance whose secrets I reveal to the audience," the magician announces. She has gotten the immediate attention of the audience, who always think they want to know exactly how the magician does every trick she shows them.

"To do this trick, all you need are two objects: a small bag and an egg." The magician displays both objects.

"At the beginning, it is important that the bag be empty on the outside (the magician shows the outside of the bag, front and back) and empty on the inside." The magician turns the bag inside out, shows both sides, and leaves it that way, inside out. "Now the inside is outside," she says, "and the outside is inside, but what's the difference?"

She puts the bag down for a moment and picks up the egg. "Now the first thing you notice about this egg," she says, "is that it isn't a real egg. It's a wooden egg." She taps it on the table a couple of times to demonstrate its woodenness. "The reason it's a wooden egg is that it was either laid by a wooden chicken, or a very angry chicken. And you'd be angry, too, if you just laid a wooden egg. Ouch!"

The magician puts the egg into the bag and says, "Now I put the egg into the bag, and I tell someone in the audience to feel that the egg is in the bag." A volunteer is recruited, who feels the egg through the cloth and testifies that the egg is in the bag.

"Next, without letting anyone see this, I take the egg from the bag and put it under my arm." The magician now holds her left arm stiffly, apparently so as not to let the egg fall.

"Then I tell the audience I'm going to make the egg vanish into thin air. I wave my hand over the bag, say the magic word—omelette—and, lo and behold, the egg vanishes." The magician turns the bag inside out and there is no egg in sight. Then she turns it back the other way.

"Of course, once in a while, you run into a skeptic who asks you to lift up your arm. If that happens, do this." The magician lifts up her right arm, meanwhile holding her left arm (the one thought to have the egg under it) stiffly. "Then again," she says, "sometimes people can be awfully insistent. Sometimes they ask that you lift *both* arms. In that case, there is really only one thing to do." The magician dramatically lifts both arms, and there is no egg to be seen.

"By now, the audience is completely baffled," says the magician. The joke is that by now the real audience is baffled. "What I usually do now is say the magic word—omelette—and if everything worked properly . . ." The magician asks a spectator to reach into the bag. A spectator reaches in and, to everyone's amazement, withdraws the wooden egg.

"Now, please," the magician asks when the applause has died down, "promise never to tell anyone how this trick is done."

The secret: This trick is one of the oldest and most prized in all of magic. There are countless variations. The fact that it is still able to fool audiences today testifies to the ability of magicians to keep a good secret.

The version of this trick described here is especially fun because, right up to the end, the audience thinks it is being let in on an inside secret. They realize only at the conclusion that they have, so to speak, been taken for a ride.

FIGURE A

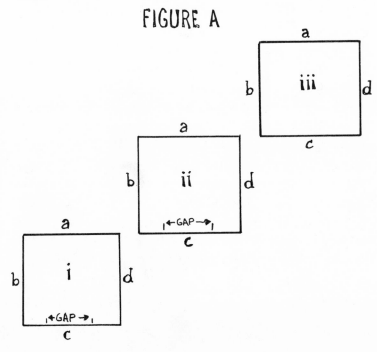

To do this trick, you will need two items: a wooden egg and a bag. Wooden eggs are often used in sewing. You could get one and paint it white. Magic supply stores carry wooden eggs. If this item is too hard to find, any rubber ball about the size of an egg will do. If you use a ball, however, be sure to call it a ball instead of an egg when you do the trick.

The bag is the magic gimmick. It is made from three pieces of thick, soft cloth (usually black or red) 7" x 8". Line up the three pieces as in Figure A: Cloth i, Cloth ii, and Cloth iii. Sew Cloth i to Cloth ii on sides a, b, c, and d, except for the 2½" gap on side c. Leave that unconnected. Then sew sides a, b, and c (including the gap area) of Cloth i to sides a, b, and c of Cloth iii, with Cloth ii in between them.

This will form a cloth bag with a secret pocket (between Cloths i and ii) and a small entrance into that secret pocket (the gap), from the bag's main pocket.

As you start the trick, the bag is turned inside out so that the gap is on the outside. The gap will not be especially visible if the bag is well made and if the bag is set on a table with the gap facing away from the audience. Show the bag's outside (really it's inside), then turn it inside out so that the gap is inside. Leave the bag this way.

Put the egg in the bag, and gingerly slip it up into the secret pocket through the gap. You will have to practice this a bit until you can do it smoothly.

Let a spectator feel the egg in the bag through the bag. It doesn't matter that the egg is in the secret pocket; it will feel the same to the spectator as if it were just an egg in a bag.

Pretend to take the egg from the bag and put it under your left arm. Actually, you leave the egg right where it is: in the bag's secret pocket. Make your left arm stiff as if it were holding the egg.

Now wave your hand over the bag and say the magic word. Show that the bag is "empty" by turning it inside out. When you turn it back the other way, smoothly slip the egg from its secret pocket back into the main pocket of the bag.

You lift your right arm, then both arms, say the magic word again, and let the spectator reach into the bag to find the egg in the main pocket.

CHAPTER TWELVE

PRACTICE MAKES BETTER

NOTHING is sadder than the sight of a panic-stricken, bewildered magician standing on stage after a trick has failed to work.

There is no way to completely guard against this. Even the best of magicians will, occasionally, fumble. However, the best way to prevent such mishaps is practice—lots of it.

Practice, they say, makes perfect. Well, at least it makes better. Like a musician or an athlete or any other skilled person, a magician must rehearse.

There are reasons that go far beyond making the trick work that should encourage a magician to practice. For example, suppose you already have practiced a trick enough to be reasonably certain that it won't fail when you go on stage.

You should continue to practice so that you can do it even more *smoothly*. Perhaps the trick works, but your *patter* is not fully coordinated with your hand movements.

Practice will improve this. While you are practicing, a new kind of patter may occur to you. An amazing number of improvements and changes in your act will occur to you while you're practicing that would never come to mind if you were just sitting back and thinking about your tricks.

The best way to approach a magic trick, when you encounter it in a book or in a set of instructions, is to read it through first so that you have a general idea of what it involves.

Having done that, you should get whatever materials the trick requires and read through the trick again, going through the motions with the appropriate props.

At this point, you are ready to begin practicing the trick seriously, going over it again and again until you have it down pat. Practicing in front of a mirror is a very good idea, because that gives you a chance to see what your movements will look like to the audience. It goes without saying that when you are practicing your trick, you should be sure that you are alone so that no one accidentally discovers your trick's secret.

Sometimes it becomes necessary, in the course of practicing a trick, to use partial self-deception. The trick described in the preceding chapter, for example, involves the magician pretending to take a wooden egg out of a bag and placing it under her arm. Actually, the egg stays hidden in the bag. In order to get that part of the trick to the point that the audience is convinced that you are doing all that, it's necessary to convince yourself that you are.

Begin by actually taking the egg out of the bag and putting it under your arm. Do that a few times. Notice how it feels and looks when you do it. Next, go through the same movements and artificially create the same sensations in your arm and in your hand just by thinking about it. If you convince yourself that you have actually taken the egg from the bag and placed it under your arm, your audience, too, will be convinced.

Once you have practiced a trick to the extent that you think you are ready to perform it smoothly, you should then think about what kind of patter or music or other effects you will add. Then you should continue to practice with these new aspects included, until everything works well together.

If your act involves an assistant (or two), you will have to include that person in your practice sessions, once you are comfortable with your own part of the trick. Stay open to an assistant's suggestions, especially when it comes to his or her own part of the trick. Sometimes, an assistant will come up with an idea or two that will make everything work more easily and may even make the trick more spectacular.

When you're pretty confident about a given trick, you should try it out in front of an informal audience before taking it on stage. Show it to a close friend or some family members in your living room, and if it goes well, you're probably ready to do it for strangers.

If, after all that practice, the trick still doesn't work when you do it on stage, don't panic. You might try for a humorous effect. Overemphasize your mistake, taking full advantage of the mishap by using it for laughs. Often, I'll just look at the fiasco, shrug, and say, "For my next trick . . ." The audience may even think you planned it as a gag.

INK YOU CAN DRINK

The effect: A magician turns a glass of ink into a glass of ordinary drinking water.

The trick: "Many, many years ago—in the Dark Ages, in fact—there was a science known as alchemy," says the magician, addressing the audience.

"The alchemists searched for ways to change inexpensive metals like lead into gold, among the most precious of elements. Did they succeed? It's hard to say. If they did, the secret is shrouded in dark mysteries, lost forever in the rush of time. *I* certainly haven't figured it out, and if I ever did, I'd buy myself an island and you'd never hear from me again.

"But I have discovered a method of transforming *certain* elements. The feat I'm about to perform would be even more valuable than the alchemists', if you ever found yourself stranded on a desert, cut off from the nearest water supply."

The magician approaches his table and says, "Somewhere here I have a glass of black ink." The magician removes an opaque cloth from its place over the glass, revealing to the audience what looks like a glass of ink. "It's a good idea to stir it up every so often," says the magician, taking a clean stick and stirring the liquid a bit. The stick emerges jet black, and the magician wipes it on a tissue, which becomes partly covered with ink.

Holding the glass aloft, the magician shows the opaque

cloth to have nothing on either side and puts it over the glass. He says a magic word or two, waves his hand over the glass, and briskly removes the cloth—to reveal that the ink has mysteriously changed to water. The magician takes a sip of water to prove that it is water and nods to the inevitable applause.

The secret: For this trick, you will need several props. You'll need a clear glass about 3½″ high and 2¼″ in diameter. You'll need an opaque cloth about a foot square, a tissue, a popsicle stick, some water, and some black ink. You'll also need to make a special gimmick.

Get a piece of thin, black plastic about 6″ x 2½″, and roll it into a cylinder (Figure A). Tape ends x and y together so that the cylinder doesn't unroll. Black plastic tape will accomplish this best.

FIGURE A

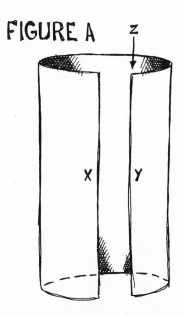

FIGURE B

FRONT   BACK

If you've done this correctly, the cylinder should slip easily into the glass. Tape a piece of black thread onto the cylinder at point z; place the cylinder into the glass and slide it all the way down to the bottom. Fill the glass with water until the cylinder is just covered. From a few feet away, it will look just as if the glass is full of ink. Let the black thread hang outside the glass.

Take the popsicle stick (without a popsicle on it, of course!), and place it in the glass. Pull it out and mark where the water comes up to on the stick. Then dry the stick off.

Cover the glass with the opaque cloth, and put it on your table on stage with the thread hidden from the audience's view partly by the cloth and partly by being put on the side of the glass that will face away from the audience. Blacken the popsicle stick with black ink up to the top of the water mark. But be sure to blacken only one side of the stick. The other side should be clear of any ink (Figure B). Allow the ink to dry. Fold the tissue and blacken it with ink on the inside of the fold so that it looks like an inky stick had been wiped off on it. Let the ink dry.

Place the stick on the table near the glass so that the clean side shows. Place the tissue nearby on the table, folded so that the ink is hidden from the audience's view. Now you are ready to begin.

Take the cloth off the glass, and show the glass to the audience. They will think it is ink. Be sure to mention ink to them *before* you take the cloth off the glass. This will plant the suggestion in their minds that what they are about to see is ink.

Place the stick in the glass, being careful not to reveal the side of the stick with the ink on it. Swish it around a little and withdraw it from the glass with the ink side to the audience, now being careful not to show the clean side of the stick to them. To the audience, it will appear as if you took a clean stick, dipped it in the ink, and got it partly covered with ink. Wipe it off on the gimmicked tissue. Before you wipe, be sure not to show the ink marks that are on the inside of the tissue. After wiping the stick, allow the ink marks to be seen. This will appear as if you have wiped an inky stick off on a clean tissue and gotten it partly covered with ink. Put the stick and the tissue out of sight and reach of the audience.

As you handle these props, pretend to be very cautious. Remember, even though you are only dealing with water, you are presenting the illusion of dealing with ink. If it really were ink, you would be very careful not to spill any or to slosh any on your clothing by mistake. You must pretend to be concerned about this with the water. You must convince the audience that it is really ink you are dealing with. Therefore, you should first more or less convince yourself. You might pretend to get a spot of ink on your hand and be very concerned about wiping it off before it dries. Don't overact, but subtly try to create the illusion that you are handling ink.

At this point, hold the glass up in your right hand and, with your left hand, put the opaque cloth over the glass. Grab onto the black thread with your left hand as you do this. After saying the magic words, smoothly pull the cloth off the glass with your left hand, all the time holding onto the thread. Under cover of the cloth, the gimmicked cylinder (which is attached to the thread) will come out of the glass. Deposit the cloth and the concealed cylinder out of sight of the audience.

When you do this, keep your eyes on the glass. Do not look at the cloth as you are pulling it off. You must practice this so that you can do it smoothly, since you will naturally want to look at the cloth and the cylinder to be sure that the trick is going all right. But if you are able to partly convince yourself that you have actually changed ink to water, you will be amazed to look at the water rather than the cloth.

Practice pulling a cloth from a plain glass of water to

see how your arm moves without the cylinder. When you are aware of just how you act when there is no cylinder involved, try to duplicate that motion when the secret cylinder is used.

CHAPTER THIRTEEN

ASSISTANTS

A MAGICIAN has so many assistants that it's impossible to count them all. From the people who manufactured the deck of cards, to the musicians who played the recorded music used in the pantomime magic, to the person who swept the stage, the magician has been assisted by more people than he or she knows.

But when we speak of a magician's assistants, we are usually talking about one of four types of helpers.

The Nonspeaking, Visible Assistant

Many magicians (usually male magicians) perform on stage with assistants who are attractive, young women in slight, tight-fitting costumes. However strange and old-fashioned this practice may appear, there is a sound theatrical reason for it. An attractive woman can very easily divert the spectator's attention from some secret maneuver the magician might be attempting.

Assistant Bonnieta Boudreau is an essential element in the magic of Carlini (Carl Blessing).

In fact, that works so well that—without making an official poll—it appears that the scantily clad, attractive woman is probably still the most commonly used type of assistant. She fits into a more general category: the non-speaking, visible assistant.

An assistant of this kind says nothing (or very little) while on stage. Mostly, he or she just carries on trays of new props and carries off trays of old ones.

While this may seem to be a rather unimportant function, you will soon discover how crucial it is if you try performing one trick with the bulky remnants of a previous trick getting in your way. If you leave a gimmicked prop lying about and a nosy spectator (children are especially

famous for this kind of meddling) happens to pick it up and look at it, the trick's secret will be revealed. Had an assistant removed the prop when the trick was over, that could have been avoided.

With this sort of assistant, his (or her) entire utility is based on performing simple tasks (like those described above) and on the way he looks.

An assistant's garb should be determined on the basis of how well it fits with the way the magician is dressed. If the magician is dressed in a traditional costume (see Chapter Three), an assistant should also dress formally but not so elegantly as to outshine the magician. Perhaps black pants and a black turtleneck shirt or sweater would work well for a male assistant. A female assistant could dress that way too, or she might wear a long fancy dress. This would give the act a consistency in elegance.

If the magician performs in a clown costume, the assistant might want to dress very plainly. Or, if the assistant chooses to dress like a clown, too, he should be a less elaborate, more ordinary clown than the magician.

It's a matter of taste, but personally I think there should be only one clown on a magician's stage, and if that clown is the magician, then the assistant should probably dress in very simple, nonclownlike attire. On the other hand, if the magician is not dressed as a clown, then a clown assistant fits almost any act. If there are two or more assistants, they might all want to dress the same way. In this case, the magician—who is dressed differently— will stand out and seem more special (magical) in contrast.

If a specific theme is established by the magician appearing as either an Oriental or East Indian, then usually the assistant will want to adhere to that theme, once again while remaining somewhat less prominent than the magician.

As in most of the other aspects of magic described in this book, there are no absolute rules about how an assistant should dress. But, generally, the assistant should keep in mind what the magician is wearing.

One additional function of the nonspeaking, visible assistant is to pretend to be very surprised when the magic happens. You will find that emotions tend to be contagious. The more surprised the assistant appears to be, the more surprised the audience will become. That will add to their enjoyment of the trick.

It should be noted that assistants should *pretend* to be surprised, because they should always be informed about how the trick works. This goes for all types of assistants except audience volunteers. The magician usually guards his secrets very carefully (Chapter Eleven), but he should always let his assistants know how the tricks are done.

The reason for this is that an assistant who does not know how a trick is done will display a natural curiosity and begin looking around in places he should not. For instance, suppose a magician has hidden a rabbit in a secret compartment in a hat. The last place the magician wants to draw the audience's attention is toward that secret compartment. An assistant is in an ideal place to notice that secret compartment. If the assistant gawks at it, it will arouse the audience's curiosity and the trick will be spoiled.

Therefore, the assistants should be briefed about how the trick is done so that they will know where *not* to look.

The Speaking, Visible Assistant

Often a magician is fortunate enough to find an assistant or assistants who are good enough performers to be given speaking parts in the show. A comedy routine could be worked out between the magician and the assistant to enhance the magic.

It is usually not a good idea to let even very personable and adept assistants actually perform any magic tricks of their own. To an audience, magic is a special power that only the magician possesses. If assistants begin displaying that power, then it seems less special, less truly magical.

But even this rule will sometimes bend under the pressure of very special circumstances.

Any performer who speaks at length in a magic show must have his or her character and on-stage personality thought out and developed. Is the assistant to be witty, stupid, a (deliberate) nuisance, a rival, or what? This should be worked out, perhaps so as to become an extension of the magician's actual relationship with the assistant off stage, perhaps not.

The Invisible Assistant

Frequently called a "plant," this kind of assistant sits out in the audience and pretends not to know the magician. An assistant of this kind can be especially helpful in a mind-reading act. Suppose you and this plant prearrange what card she will pick from a deck. Then, during the performance, if this assistant—who appears to be a volunteer from the audience—picks that card, the magician should have no trouble figuring out which one it is.

There are drawbacks to using this kind of hidden assistant. For one thing, audiences suspect this sort of collusion. Another problem is that you can't usually use a plant when you are performing for a small group or for friends. The plant will just appear too obvious.

The Audience Volunteer

Many tricks call for the magician to ask for help from a spectator in the audience. These kinds of tricks are usually very effective, especially if the magician gets lucky and the spectator is an interesting person. Sometimes, a magician will select a volunteer and joke with him or her a bit before getting to the actual feat of magic.

Children very often make the best volunteers, and if you perform for an audience mostly composed of kids, you will find that your biggest problem will be in selecting

Trying out a new trick, novice magician H. M. Steiger III gets a little help from a puppet-assistant.

just one volunteer from an entire audience that is anxious to come up on stage to help you. (For this reason, when performing for children, it's a good idea to select several tricks that require audience volunteers, or a trick that requires several audience volunteers.)

On the other hand, if your audience is mainly composed of adults, you may find it tough to get people to volunteer. If you must pick someone, do so pleasantly but firmly. If someone is reluctant to come and help, perhaps audience applause will serve as encouragement. If the person is too reluctant, find someone else.

Often when I perform I bring some lightweight juggling balls with me. I juggle them for a moment and then toss a ball into the audience. Whoever catches it is asked to bring it up to me on stage. Then, while she's there, I ask her to assist me in a trick. This also reduces the possibility, in the minds of the audience, of collusion between us, since the selection was as random as the toss of a ball.

While a volunteer is assisting you, always remember to be very courteous, saying "thank you" and "please" and so on. You might poke a little fun at a spectator, but always do so politely.

After a volunteer has assisted you in a trick, always be sure to thank her for her help. A small gift, especially one magically produced, is a nice way to say thanks.

ONE PLUS ONE EQUALS ONE

The effect: A spectator ties two ropes together, and the magician magically joins them together into one piece of rope.

The trick: The magician enters with two thin pieces of rope, each of which appears to be about a foot long. "I've got two pieces of rope here," says the magician, "that are about the same length. Would someone help me by tying them together?"

A spectator is selected, and he ties the two ropes together tightly at one end. The magician then asks the spectator to tie the two free ends of rope together. Next, the magician withdraws a pair of scissors from her pocket and hands it to the spectator telling him to point to one end.

One end is then cut off by the spectator. This leaves one piece of rope, in effect, joined in the middle by a knot. The magician places the scissors back in her pocket and wraps the rope around her hand. She once again takes the scissors from her pocket and waves them over the rope, which is still wound about her hand.

The magician asks the spectator to take hold of the free end of the rope and to unwind it from her hand. The rope is unwound only to be found to be one long, smooth, unknotted piece of rope, which may be examined by the spectator.

The secret: Before facing an audience, take a 24" piece of rope and cut it into two very uneven pieces of rope, one about 4" long and the other about 20" long.

Fold each piece in half, thread one inside the other, and hold them as in Figure A. To the audience, it will appear that the magician is holding two pieces of rope, each of which is about a foot long. Squeeze the ropes tightly at junction X, and ask the spectator to double knot the rope at that end. Be careful, as you do this, to hold the junction

FIGURE A

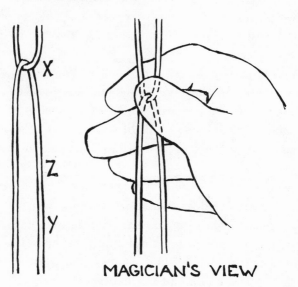

MAGICIAN'S VIEW

tightly between your thumb and forefinger so that no one sees it.

Let the knot be tied just above junction X so that, when the end is released, it looks very much like a knot has been tied in two ropes of even length.

Hold the ropes at point Y and pinch them together there. Have the spectator double knot the ropes there, also.

Hold the ropes casually at point Z and ask the spectator to point to one end. You must force him to choose to cut off end Y while giving him the illusion of free choice. Do that in this way: If he points to end Y, say, "Fine. Would you cut off that end, please?" If he points to end X, say, "Very good. We'll save that end. Would you cut off this end (end Y) please?" It always works because the spectator does not know in advance just why he is pointing to an end: to choose an end to save or an end to cut off. Also, be sure to say "point to" and not "pick." The former is more vague than the latter and, therefore, better for our purposes here.

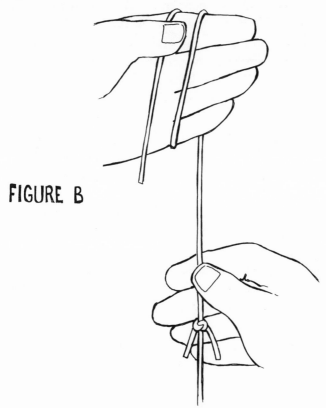

FIGURE B

Once end Y has been cut off, give it to the spectator to keep as a souvenir. Next, let the rope unfold so that the audience sees you have one long rope, tied in the middle.

Hold the rope in the left hand between the thumb and first finger, letting it drape down in front of the fingers, and wind it around the left hand with the right (Figure B). As you wind the rope, you will come to the knot. It will simply slip down the rope as you slide it with your right hand. Do not let the audience see you doing this. Hide the motion with your right hand. The audience will simply assume that the knot is out of sight, still on the rope in the palm of the left hand. Actually, you slide it off and hide it in the palm of the right hand.

After the spectator has cut the rope, you returned the scissors to your pocket. Reach for the scissors again with the right hand, secretly depositing the knot in the pocket as you do so.

All that is left is to wave the scissors over the left hand (and the rope) and to have the spectator unwind the rope from that hand.

Thank the spectator who helped you, and as he returns to his seat, ask the audience to join you in thanking him with a round of applause.

CHAPTER FOURTEEN

OTHER WIZARDS

HAVE you ever wished that you could get together with a group of other magicians to trade secrets and talk to each other about your experiences in magic? Well, you know, there's nothing stopping you from doing that. All you've got to do is meet another magician, and the two of you are sure to have a lot to talk about. If a few of your friends are interested in magic, you can even start your own magic club.

In your magic club, you can make your own rules. You can plan your own special events like a super magic show to help raise money for the club. All of the club's members might want to use the same kind of magic wands when you have your club meetings. You might want to call each other by your special magic names only.

You can learn a lot about magic by talking to other magicians and comparing notes. You can learn new tricks, new ways to perform old tricks, interesting and amusing touches to add to tricks, and much more.

Instead of forming your own magic club, you might

want to join one that has already been set up. There are many such clubs, but the two largest are the Society of American Magicians (SAM) and the International Brotherhood of Magicians (IBM). To join either of these organizations, you must be at least eighteen years old, but many of their local chapters have junior clubs that are open to kids who are at least fourteen years old (see Appendix II).

In October 1979, Ring (chapter) 12 of the IBM held a magic convention in Niagara Falls, NY. It was called a "NYCAN" and was organized by Howard Eldridge, a magician from Buffalo, NY. Magicians came to this meeting from all over the United States and Canada for 3 days of magical events. This convention was just one of the many conclaves magicians hold each year. Meetings like these are among the principal methods through which magicians stay in touch with each other and share their discoveries in the world of magic.

You may not be a member of such a large magical organization, but if you and some friends wanted to hold your own magic convention, there is no reason why you couldn't. It wouldn't be as large or grand as those of the IBM, but with a little work it could be a lot of fun.

What goes on at a magic convention?

The one in Niagara Falls was pretty typical, and it included a variety of activities.

There were several magic shows on stage in which many of the magicians attending the convention participated. Sometimes these shows were open to the general public, sometimes only club members were allowed to see them.

Experienced magicians gave lectures to the conventioneers in which they shared their painstakingly acquired knowledge about various forms of magic.

One day, magicians who specialize in close-up magic (such as coin tricks and card tricks) put on close-up shows in small rooms for limited audiences.

Magic shops from around the country sent representatives to the convention. These magic dealers set up their booths at the convention and sold their special magical equipment.

The convention also included business meetings (in which the immediate business of the club was discussed), a banquet (at which those members who did special work for the club were honored), and parties (just for fun).

If you, together with some of your friends who are interested in magic, decide to hold your own magic convention, you might want to include some of these events.

The most important part of the convention in Niagara Falls was the opportunity it presented to meet with other magicians and talk about magic.

One magician at the convention, Emil Loew, was almost 70 years old. He had grown up in the Netherlands and had been living in New York City since 1940. Like most magicians, he started in magic when he was a child. In fact, he remembered that he was just 9 years old when he did his first magic tricks.

"I was sick at that time," he said. "I had just about every child's disease that there is at the same time. My mother wanted to keep me both busy and interested."

So, he continued, she brought him magic trick after magic trick, and he's been a magician ever since.

Jimmie Lake, a magician from Scarborough, Ontario, was also in attendance. His story was a little different. "All of us, as kids, learn a couple of magic tricks," he said. But he never seriously studied magic until he was much older and married. "My wife and I formed a bridge club. They were very popular at the time. They were a fad," he recalled. One night, after a particularly fun game of bridge, a strange memory flew into his head. "I suddenly thought of these card tricks I learned as a kid."

He performed the tricks for his friends and although, he admitted, the tricks were pretty simple and his presentation a little shaky, the impromptu performance was a big hit. "It got so that every week they waited for me to do a new card trick. I went to the library and got some books of card tricks and studied them so I could surprise my friends every week."

From there, Jimmie Lake went on to become one of the most respected magicians in Canada. He offered some advice for young people who are just starting out as magicians.

"One common mistake that they make is that they don't talk loudly enough. They whisper. I tell them to speak to the people in the back row of the room. Another fault is that they're always turning their backs on the audience. There was one guy, we saw more of his back than his front," he said.

Chris Buck—a young woman from Rochester, NY who has been a magician for 3 years—has other advice for beginners. "Make sure you're really interested in magic before you get into it. And you can't be shy. You don't need to spend a lot of money on your tricks, either. You can make a lot of your own things. You should be creative," she said.

Traditionally, more men than women have become magicians, but this didn't bother Chris at all. "It's just something I was interested in, so I thought that I'd give it a shot. But, you know, since I've gotten into it, I've realized that there are a lot more women magicians than I thought."

Linda Harle-Mould is a magician who lectured at the Niagara Falls meeting. She's from Taneytown, MD and her story is very unusual. "I started in magic when I was 2 years old," she said. Her father is a magician known as "Uncle Harry." She began as a baby, assisting him on stage. "When I was little, my job was catching silks out of productions and having things handed to me. Starting so very young meant that I stopped being afraid of an audience very early."

As she grew older, she found herself becoming more and more involved in her father's act. Soon she, too, wanted to *be* the magician, instead of only assisting.

In the meantime, she also became an ordained minister in the United Church of Christ and she married a man who is also a minister. Today, she works both as a religious leader and as a magician, often combining the two. And, in a reversal of traditional sex roles, Rev. Harle-Mould says that she is currently training her husband to be her assistant.

Going to a magic convention is a way of sharing your secrets of magic with other magicians. But it's also a way of getting a broader perspective not only on magic but on people in general. It's a way of sharing your observations with other people who are interested in some of the same things that you are. By the way, it's fun, too!

PART

VI

GETTING READY

Having learned the tricks and practiced the patter, the magician can still give a show that is a disorganized nightmare. Even if the show is a good one, it doesn't mean a thing unless the magician gets a chance to perform it.

In Chapter Fifteen, the method of drawing together the various elements of magic into one cohesive show are discussed. Then, in Chapter Sixteen, the means of letting the public know about your show are examined in some detail.

PUTTING A SHOW TOGETHER

ACTUALLY putting together a magic show can be a lot more work than learning any of the individual tricks in that show.

Let's assume that you've learned the tricks that you want to put in your show, and you've been promised an opportunity to perform that show sometime in the near future. You've still got quite a bit of planning to do and a number of decisions to make.

Your first decision is how long you want your show to be. These days magic shows seldom run longer than an hour. If your audience is mostly children, then between a half hour and 45 minutes is usually an adequate length. Try not to give yourself too much to do at first, especially if you haven't given many (or any) magic shows before.

The show should have an overall logic or theme to it. Even though it is composed of individual tricks, the entire presentation should fit together and should make sense as a cohesive entity. The personality or character you create on stage should remain consistent throughout the entire program. If your on-stage personality is humorous, for example, then it should be consistently humorous.

It wouldn't make much sense for you to be an oriental magician in your first trick and an ancient wizard in your second one. You may, however, easily assume features of each in turn, to give each trick its own special character.

Sometimes you might find that two tricks fit together very well, so you should do them one after the other in your show. Two rope tricks—each of which might take 5 minutes to perform—might be blended into one gala rope trick that would take about 10 minutes. A trick like Thirsty (Chapter Ten), in which a glass of milk is created from thin air, might be good to perform after the Vanishing Milk Pitcher (available from most magic stores and catalogs), in which milk vanishes into thin air.

Experiment and see which tricks go well together. It's important to think of the show's parts as belonging to the show as a whole.

A good general rule regarding your show is to always open with a quick, snappy trick. This trick, which could be done silently as you walk on stage to a musical accompaniment, immediately sets the tone for the show and establishes you in the minds of the spectators as a magician.

You might think it best to end with your most spectacular feat of magic. Actually, it's best to have your next to the last trick be your biggest and most spectacular trick.

Your last trick should be a shorter, somewhat humorous trick that sort of says, "Goodbye. See you soon." If you

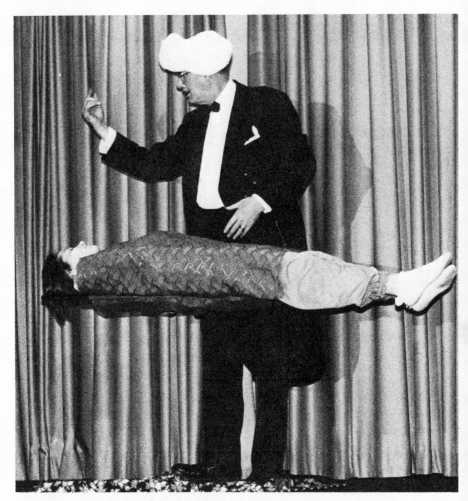

Akbar (Frank Hayes) accomplishes the traditional "floating lady" effect, with a little help from Kathy Yff.

are performing for children, it is often a good idea if your last trick is one in which you magically produce little treats or favors for the youngsters to take home with them. An example of this kind of trick is provided later in this chapter.

Marvo (Myron Ortolano) concentrates as he prepares for his act's finale.

When you rehearse your show as a whole, practice going smoothly from one trick to the next. Work out a system so that if you need a table or a work space to perform a trick, it is not cluttered with props from a preceding or upcoming trick.

Since it is likely that you will change the number and arrangement of your tricks from show to show, it's a good idea to write down the order of the tricks for each show on a small card (a 3″ x 5″ index card works well). Put that card in a convenient but inconspicuous place on one of your tables. You and your assistant(s) can consult this list from time to time to see what trick is to be done next.

Always have more tricks ready to perform than you intend to use and try to stay flexible. If something goes wrong with a scheduled trick, you can always substitute one of these extra tricks in its place. Also, after planning to perform a half hour show, you may find that you've been performing too quickly and that the show looks as if it will be over in 20 minutes. Here again, the extra tricks will come in handy.

Once you have definitely concluded a show and have taken your final bows, however, don't do any additional tricks. Resist, even if the audience begs you for more. (And here, too, there are exceptions to this rule.) Never cheat an audience, but always leave them wanting more. That way, they will ask you back to perform again.

THE PAPER CONFECTIONERY

The effect: The magician changes some paper confetti into candy.

The trick: The magician brings out a glass and a box. The glass is empty, and the box is full of confetti. The magician displays the glass clearly and dips her hand into the box and pulls out a handful of confetti, which she tosses into the air.

She dips the glass into the box a few times, each time filling it with more and more confetti, until it is brimming full to overflowing. She brushes a mound of excess confetti off the top of the glass so that the confetti level is even with the top of the glass.

The magician picks up an opaque cloth and shows it to be empty. She covers the glass of confetti with the cloth, says a magic word or two, and removes the cloth. The confetti has changed to candy.

The secret: This trick is a good one to perform at the end of a show, especially a show for children.

To do this trick, you will need a lot of confetti, two identical glasses, about 5″ tall and 2½″ in diameter, an opaque box to hold the confetti (about a foot cube), some candy, and a special gimmick.

You can make this gimmick by getting a piece of thin cardboard or poster board about 9″ x 4½″. Roll it into a cylinder, and tape it securely so that the cylinder doesn't unroll. It should fit very smoothly and easily into the glasses and extend inside either glass from the bottom of the glass to the top, but not beyond the rim.

Cut a circle of poster board that is slightly (about ¼″) larger in diameter than the glass. Tape the poster board circle to one end of the cylinder as in Figure A.

Next, you will need confetti, which you can make by

FIGURE A

FIGURE B

cutting up newspapers (the colored comic section is best) or just cutting up multicolored construction paper. Glue confetti onto the outside of the cylinder and the top of the poster board circle until none of the poster board is showing. Put the rest of the confetti in the box.

Place the cylinder/circle on a table so that the circle part rests on the table. Fill the cylinder part with candy. Use prewrapped candy to avoid transmitting unnecessary germs.

Place the glass, mouth down, on top of the cylinder until the cylinder is completely covered with the glass. Turn this whole thing rightside up (Figure B). You will notice that from a distance this looks like a glass full of confetti.

Place this glass and gimmick in the box. The box should be tall enough so that the audience will not be able to see the gimmicked glass inside the box.

Get a second, empty glass and you are ready to begin.

Display the empty glass to the audience. Reach into the box and pull out some confetti and throw it into the air.

Cradling the box in your left arm, with your right hand dip the empty glass into the box filling it about halfway full with confetti. Pull the partially full glass out of the box, all in one smooth motion. Repeat this motion, this time filling the glass up all the way.

On your third pass with the glass into the box, let go of the glass and pick up the glass with the gimmick in it. Practice this switching so that you make the transition smoothly. To the audience it should appear that you still have the same glass in your hand. As you bring the gimmicked glass out of the box, scoop up some additional confetti on top of the poster board circle (which is, of course, already covered with glued-on confetti).

Show this glass to the audience and neatly brush the extra confetti back into the box.

Put the box down on a table behind you, out of easy sight of the audience, but well within your reach. Holding the gimmicked glass in your left hand, pick up an opaque cloth in your right hand and display both sides.

Place it over the glass. You will find that you can easily feel the rim of the gimmicked, poster board circle since it extends slightly beyond the glass rim.

Say a magic word and pull out the poster board cylinder/circle under cover of the cloth. Discard the gimmick and cloth in the box. Do this nonchalantly, not looking at the cloth, gimmick, or box. Fix your gaze instead on the glass in your hand, which is now magically full of candy, seemingly transformed from the confetti.

It is very important, especially with children, that every single child get a piece of candy. Unfortunately, it may be hard to get enough pieces of candy into the cylinder gimmick.

Here's a little trick to solve that problem. Get an opaque dish and fill it partway with candy. Make sure that the dish is deep enough and big enough so that the audience can not easily see into it.

After you have produced the candy in the glass, pour that candy into the dish, where it will mingle with the extra candy that is already there. That way, every child will get a piece of candy and each piece will seem specially created, as if by magic. In fact, it's probably a good idea to keep several additional pieces of candy in a bag backstage, just in case. Should you somehow miscalculate, this will avoid any child being neglected.

CHAPTER SIXTEEN

PUBLICITY

W HEN you've got a terrific magic show, you want people to see that show. But no matter how good a show you've developed, no one will ever see it unless you take steps to publicize it.

A small one-person (or two-person) magic show does not have a great deal of money to publicize itself. What is lacking in budget must be made up for in ingenuity. There are a variety of free or inexpensive ways to call attention to your show.

A SMALL AD. One way to make a large number of people aware of your act relatively quickly is to take an ad in a newspaper. Generally, a small newspaper is better than a large one. People tend to pay more attention to an ad of this kind that they see in a friendly community paper than to one they see in a big impersonal publication. Local newsletters and religious publications—if they accept ads —will frequently yield good results. An ad in a small publication is also usually less of a financial risk to you than an ad in a large periodical.

The way advertising generally works is that people usually won't respond unless they see the same thing advertised several times. For this reason, it is a good idea to let your ad run in the same publication for a little while before becoming discouraged and trying something else.

The ad should include your stage name, your telephone number, and a brief statement of what it is you do. Since most people don't spend a lot of time reading ads (and since most publications charge for their ads by the word), you will generally want to keep your ad as concise as possible.

An example might run something like this: "Magic Shows For Children's Birthday Parties by The Amazing Alberti. Entertainment Extraordinaire. Phone 999–0000."

It also helps to encourage people to hire you if they hear about you from several different sources. That's why it's a good idea to use several (if not all) of the methods suggested here, as well as any others you may be able to think of yourself.

FLYERS AND PROGRAMS. Once you have been scheduled to perform a magic show somewhere, you should realize that if there are 20 people in the audience, then that means there are 20 potential customers there who might want you to perform at a party or special event. But they won't do that unless they know how to contact you easily.

One way to accomplish this is to make up a mimeographed, dittoed, or photocopied flyer or program and hand one out to each member of the audience.

Such a program should contain some interesting cover design that is easily associated in the minds of most people with magic. Rabbits, top hats, magic wands, fans of cards, puffs of smoke, streaks of lightning: All of these items mean magic to most people. If you are a good artist, then draw the design yourself. If not, get an artist friend to help.

The cover should also contain your stage name. Magicians have traditionally been extremely immodest in their publicity devices. If you really could do all the things that you only seem to do in your act, then it would be well within reason to command such unusually complimentary publicity. It is all part of the illusion that you are a kind of miracle worker.

Many magicians also want to add to their program cover some title or appellation in addition to their name. If the magician does mostly card tricks, he might call himself, "The King of Cards." If she does mostly coin magic, then "The Queen of Coins" might be more appropriate. A magician who specializes in escapes could call himself, "Escape Artist, Extraordinaire," while a mind reader might be dubbed, "Mentalist Supreme."

It is also a good idea to let people know somewhere on your program what you are doing in general. An example of what you might write would go something like, "The Amazing Alberti's performance features astounding and incredible feats of hocus-pocus and sleight of hand guaranteed to baffle even the most careful observer of magic."

Inside, the program should contain a listing of the tricks you expect to perform. One drawback to this is that a magician frequently changes his program from show to show. For this reason, many magicians elect to just prepare a flyer telling a little about themselves and to distribute this at the end of the act. (A program should be distributed at the start of the show.)

Another solution is to list your entire repertoire of tricks and then to add a line above the list saying, "The Amazing Alberti's program includes several incredible feats of magic selected from among those listed below."

The tricks should all be given exciting and interesting names to pique the curiosity of the audience. However, the name should not tell too much about the trick. Very often a trick works best if the audience doesn't know exactly what to expect. If the audience is kept in the dark that you are going to, for example, cut and restore a rope, then they won't know exactly what gimmick to watch for as you do your trick. Besides, One Plus One Equals One is more intriguing a name for a trick than Cut and Restored Rope.

You may want to add a line or two about each trick to further spark curiosity, but, once again, do not tell too much about the trick. For One Plus One Equals One, do not say, "A trick in which two separate pieces of rope become one." Instead, write something like, "A fascinating illusion which has astounded the crowned heads of Europe. Magic with a rope gleaned from the lore of the Indian fakirs defying all laws of mathematics and physics."

The program should also contain a very prominent notice stating your telephone number. It is probably best not to list your prices, since they could vary greatly depending on the circumstances.

PERSONAL CONTACTS. Do not be afraid to tell people you know personally about yourself and to try to interest them in a magic show if you know they are planning a party in the near future. You could have inexpensive business cards printed up to give to people you know to remind them that you are in the business of doing magic.

When you are just starting out, this kind of advertising is especially important.

POSTERS. If you are scheduled to do a show that is open to the public, you should make some posters to help advertise and bring people in. If you are performing publicly under the auspices of a school, church, or other group, they may be willing to supply you with materials to make the posters if you are sure to mention the group's name.

In making the posters, you will want to follow many of the same general techniques that you used in designing your program cover.

S–T–R–E–T–C–H–I–N–G IT

The effect: The magician stretches a small, borrowed business card around the waist of a spectator.

The trick and secret: This is less of a real magic trick than it is a little joke or puzzle. It is an inventive way of spreading your name around for publicity purposes.

Ask a potential employer (or friend) for her business card. (In case she doesn't have one, any card will do: an index card, or even a playing card, as long as she doesn't

FIGURE A

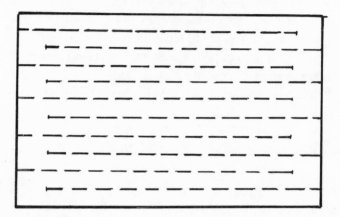

need to have it back.) Bet her that you can stretch that card (which, if it is a standard business card, probably measures 3½″ x 2″) around her waist. To do this, simply cut the card as indicated in Figure A, cutting on the dotted lines. The resulting string of card will fit around the waist of even your fattest friend or acquaintance.

Before leaving her, thank her for the use of her business card. And, while you're at it, offer her one of yours.

And, if she ever needs a magician . . .

CONCLUSION

THIS book has mainly tried to give you some ideas about creating and organizing a full-scale magic show of a manageable size. But the book has been about more than that. It's been about being a magician.

You'll find that once you've begun performing your own magic show on a regular basis, the fact that you are a magician will begin to mean more and more to you. It will even affect other areas of your life.

The matter of practice (Chapter Twelve), for example, may quickly have an effect on your school work. There are few disciplines as demanding as those involved in learning a difficult magic trick. While most of the illusions described in this book can be mastered relatively quickly with some serious practice, other magic tricks you will soon encounter will demand even more of your time and concentration, just to master their mechanics. The habits of practice that you'll develop in learning these tricks will help you in learning other skills in school, and elsewhere.

Mastering the problems involved in speaking to your audience from the stage will help you to build self-confidence in dealing with other people. Learning to be at ease with your own personality while you are under the scrutiny of an audience will teach you that composure in your appearance is as important when working with others as anything you may have to say.

Working as a magician combines the skills of an actor, a writer, a director, a designer, and a producer. This firsthand experience, even though it's on a small scale, should give you a keener appreciation of theater in general. As a member of the audience at a play, for example, you will—if you are a magician—have a pretty good idea of what is involved in staging such a production and of what the whole thing looks like from the other side of the footlights.

You may find that whole new ways of looking at a play —or at another magician's show, for that matter—will suggest themselves to you. As a junior member of the twin worlds of entertainment and art, you will view those worlds as an insider. This will probably make you both more tolerant of the faults of other entertainers and more intelligently critical in terms of assessing the merits of a particular production.

Perhaps the biggest effect that being a magician can have on a person comes in the matter of "secrets" (Chapter Eleven). In fact, it may be that people who become magicians have rather secretive personalities to begin with, and that's one reason why they become magicians in the first place.

Be that as it may, it's generally true that once you've been a magician for a while, your relationship to "secrets" changes. Being able to keep a secret is so important to a magician that you usually become pretty good at it. Not only do you become more trustworthy but you develop a turn of mind that allows you to stand apart from others in certain matters. The special knowledge that you acquire to perform your tricks and the air of mystery you cultivate to make the tricks seem more amazing may begin to encourage a certain independence. When you've got secrets, after all, you can't go off sharing them with everybody, or they won't be secrets for long.

Much of what I've been talking about so far is pretty speculative and may vary greatly from individual to individual. Still, there are some changes in your life that almost certainly go with being a magician.

Most important among these is that at gatherings of friends and family a person who is a magician is almost certain to be asked—on the spur of the moment—to do some magic tricks. Once it's known that you are a magician and that you often perform magic shows, this will unquestionably begin happening to you, too.

While this book has most often been concerned with magic that can be performed in the context of a planned, formal magic show, it will be important for you to be willing and able (and, perhaps, eager) to perform tricks of a more spontaneous nature. This is, in a way, something that a magician owes to the world. If you are a miracle worker, then you should be able to do your miracles at any time in any place.

Most of the tricks described—for example, those in Chapters Two, Six, Seven, and Sixteen—can be performed without any preparation, with materials found easily in most homes. Other tricks, such as those described in Chapters Nine and Thirteen, will require a bit of preparation, but they can also be performed with easily found materials at a few moments' notice.

You'll find that performing magic in impromptu situations is rather different from working within the structures of a formal magic show. The conditions of impromptu magic are harder to control; you must be able to improvise, to think on your feet. The audience, too, will generally be less aware of the boundaries between the performer and themselves. They are generally more talkative, less respectful. You are not, in their eyes, someone who has worked hard to prepare yourself to entertain them. You're just someone who, for the moment, is trying to trick them.

In an impromptu performance, you must be careful to remain in control of the moment, to keep a certain order and logic to your performance. Whatever you do, don't perform too many tricks in an impromptu setting; one or two are enough.

You also will have to adjust your patter and your performing personality to the informality of the situation. You can't be as theatrical in an impromptu performance as you are in a stage magic show. Your stage personality must be relaxed and toned down a little to fit the less rigid, more personal situation. If your stage personality is basically an extension of your day-to-day personality, then it will be easy for you to just relax slightly and slip into a more natural manner for an impromptu performance.

However, if you have devised a highly unusual stage personality for yourself, then it may be necessary to develop a more natural personality—one that is closer to your real personality—for use in spontaneous performances.

In any case, impromptu magic will often be requested and you should be prepared to deliver. Magic is to most people, if not a wonderful adventure, at least a lot of fun. And it's hard for most people who find themselves with a magician in their midst to let him or her go without performing at least one trick. Just one, please.

That is where I'll leave you, for now. If you've read this book carefully, you've got not only a bag of tricks but a pretty good idea about how to begin to use those tricks.

Being a magician doesn't mean devoting all your time to magic. It doesn't mean neglecting your school work, your family, or your friends. Rather, being a magician means staying with magic, putting some effort into it, and thinking about new ways of presenting your illusions. It means giving some thought to the art of magic. And it means giving some time to magic when you're in the right frame of mind, and sometimes when you're not.

But I probably don't even have to tell you that. After all, if you've read this book, then you may already be a magician.

MAGIC SUPPLIES

All of the special equipment you will need for the tricks described in this book are things you can make yourself, rather inexpensively. But you may want to buy some magical supplies that you can't make yourself, and that's where magic shops come in.

The following list contains some of the shops around the country. Consult the yellow pages of your telephone book under headings like "Magicians' Supplies" and "Magicians" to find other nearby shops.

Many magic shops will send you catalogs that tell you what kinds of tricks they have in stock. Write to them requesting a catalog. In many cases, you can even order your magical supplies by mail.

Abbott's Magic Manufac-
  turing Co.
Colom, MI 49040

Al's Magic Shop
1205 Pennsylvania Ave., NW
Washington, DC 20004

S.S. Adams Co.
P.O. Box 369
Neptune, NJ 07753

Berg's Magic Studio
6560 Hollywood Blvd.
Hollywood, CA 90028

D. Robbins and Co.
127 W. 17th St.
New York, NY 10011

Devoe Magic Den
109 N. 7th St.
St. Louis, MO 63101

Ed Drane Co.
1400 N. Halstead
Chicago, IL 60622

E.M.I. Magic
45 Main St.
Tonawanda, NY 14150

Fabjance Studios
Box 123
Bethalto, IL 62010

Guaranteed Magic
27 Bright Rd.
Hatboro, PA 19040

Haines House of Cards
2465 Williams Ave.
Cincinnati, OH 45212

House of Hocus Pocus
1667 Hertel Ave.
Buffalo, NY 14216

Owen Magic Supreme
1240 S. Chapel Ave.
Alhambra, CA 91801

Paul's Magic and Fun Shop
903 N. Federal Hwy.
Ft. Lauderdale, FL 33306

Presley Guitar Creations
P.O. Box 2279
Abilene, TX 79604

Silk King Studios
640 Evening Star Lane
Cincinnati, OH 45220

Tannen's Magic, Inc.
1540 Broadway
New York, NY 10036

MAGICIANS' ORGANIZATIONS

You and a few friends can form your own magic club. But if you want to know about some larger magical organizations, there are at least two important ones.

The Society of American Magicians (SAM) is the oldest magicians' organization in the world, while the International Brotherhood of Magicians (IBM) is the largest. In most cases, you must be 18 years old to join, but many local chapters—called Assemblies or Rings—have junior clubs open to kids who are 14 years and older.

You can contact the main headquarters of those clubs at these addresses:

Society of American Magicians
c/o Herbert B. Downs
66 Marked Tree Rd.
Needham, MA 02192

International Brotherhood of Magicians
114 N. Detroit St.
Kenton, OH 43326

III MAGIC PERIODICALS

Magicians' magazines help to keep you up to date in the world of magic, provide valuable information, and often contain the secrets to fascinating illusions.

The Society of American Magicians publishes a periodical called *Magic—Unity—Might*. It's available to members only. For further information, write to the Society of American Magicians, c/o Herbert B. Downs, 66 Marked Tree Rd., Needham, MA 02192.

The International Brotherhood of Magicians also publishes a periodical called *The Linking Ring*, which is available to members only. For further information, write to the International Brotherhood of Magicians, 114 N. Detroit St., Kenton, OH 43326.

Other periodicals, available to all interested magicians, are:

Tops Magazine
c/o Abbott's Magic Manufac-
    turing Co.
Colom, MI 49040

Genii Magazine
P.O. Box 36068
Los Angeles, CA 90036

Hocus Pocus
c/o The Magic Towne
    House
1026 3rd Ave.
New York, NY 10021

SUGGESTED FURTHER READINGS

Arnold, Ned, and Arnold, Lois. *The Great Science Magic Show.* New York: Franklin Watts, 1979.

Blackstone, Harry. *Blackstone's Modern Card Tricks.* North Hollywood, Calif.: Wilshire Book Co., 1974.

Christopher, Milbourne. *Panorama of Magic.* New York: Dover, 1962.

Dolan, Edward B., Jr. *The Complete Beginner's Guide to Magic.* Garden City, N.Y.: Doubleday, 1977.

Dunninger, Joseph. *Dunninger's Complete Encyclopedia of Magic.* Secaucus, N.J.: Lyle Stuart, 1967.

———. *One Hundred Classic Houdini Tricks You Can Do.* New York: Arco Publishing Co., 1975.

Elliott, Bruce. *Classic Secrets of Magic.* New York: Collier, 1962.

———. *Magic as a Hobby.* New York: Gramercy, 1948.

Evans, Henry. *History of Conjuring and Magic.* New York: Gordon Press.

Feinman, Jeffrey. *Magic: One Hundred Ninety-Three Easy-to-Do, Impossible to Detect Magic Tricks.* New York: Wanderer Books, 1980.

Fulves, Karl. *Self-Working Card Tricks: Seventy-Two Foolproof Card Miracles for the Amateur Magician.* New York: Dover Publications, 1976.

Gibson, Walter. *Card Magic Made Easy.* New York: Barnes & Noble, 1976.

Hay, Henry. *The Amateur Magician's Handbook.* New York: New American Library, 1974.

McGill, Ormond. *Entertaining with Magic.* Cranbury, N.J.: A.S. Barnes, 1976.

Scarne, John. *Scarne on Card Tricks.* New York: Crown, 1950.

Selbit, H. *The Magician's Handbook and Encyclopedia.* New York: Gordon Press Pubs., 1976.

Seuling, Barbara. *Abracadabra: Creating Your Own Magic Show from Beginning to End.* New York: Julian Messner, 1975.

Severn, Bill. *Magic Comedy Tricks, Skits & Clowning.* New York: David McKay, 1968.

Stoddard, Edward. *The First Book of Magic.* New York: Franklin Watts, 1967.

White, Laurence B., Jr. *So You Want to Be a Magician?* Reading, Mass.: Addison-Wesley Publishing Co., 1972.

INDEX

ABOUT THE AUTHOR

Ever since he was a little boy, Jay Boyar has been performing, watching, and thinking about magic.

He was born in Brooklyn, New York, in 1953 and soon came to develop an unusual interest in magic tricks of all kinds, particularly magic with coins and cards. As a child, he also realized that by concentrating intently on a trick he'd just been shown, he could generally figure out how it was done without being told. This initial fascination with magic tricks *as puzzles to be solved* soon lead to a desire to approach magic *as a theatrical art form.*

Beginning with ad-hoc performances for his family, he soon graduated to small shows for neighborhood kids in his parents' garage. By the time he entered college—where he studied English literature—he was supporting himself as a magician.

In college, writing—and journalism, in particular—became increasingly attractive to him as a career. He served as Arts Editor on his student newspaper. Upon graduation, the paper's staff presented him with a "sword-through-the-neck" illusion, which they'd purchased especially for him from a nearby magic shop.

After college, he spent nearly two years on the staff of the New York *Post* and has since written for a variety of newspapers and magazines, as well as for radio and television stations. Currently, he writes regularly about the arts in Buffalo,

New York, for the *Courier-Express* and is a Contributing Editor for *Spree* magazine. Magic is a frequent topic of his journalistic explorations.

Jay Boyar has taught magic on and off for nearly a decade, both to individual students and in classroom settings. This book has grown directly from those lessons and incorporates ideas suggested by the questions and observations of his many students. He is currently at work on a book about the history of the movies, also for Julian Messner.